Online Publishing –
Do it yourself

Alberto García Briz

Online Publishing – Do it yourself

Alberto García Briz

First edition – December 2014

Translation from the original "**Publicación Online – hazlo tú mismo**", 4th **ed.**, in Spanish language

Paperback version:

ISBN-13: 978-1491296844 (CreateSpace)

ISBN-10: 1491296844

Translation and cover design by Alberto García Briz

For all these people who have a book draft in some drawer...

Contents

Introduction

Since August 2012, one of my main activities during my leisure time has been, together with photography, online publication. So far you may find just a few books published (both in Spanish and English), being this one my most recent proposal.

Of course, I have been bugging my family and friends with news, messages and updates on my progress. Later on I will tell you a couple of things on promotion.

However, I am happy to say that I reached a reasonable level of sales outside my circles. Nothing spectacular, but I also did not expect to get rich with this...

What I did find is that a lot of people has some idea in their minds, some abandoned (or not) projects in a drawer, maybe written on small notebooks or just in their minds.

I guess a few years ago you could speak about sloth, or rather about the complication in approaching a "real" editor to publish your book. Minimum printing series were maybe a few thousands of books, which implied some non-negligible costs... Currently, you can print a single book, if this is what you want. Or half a dozen, for family and friends.

Yes, it is really easy to publish "almost" anything. Of course, no editor (either for paperback or electronic version) will typically accept any publication with racist or illegal contents. However, a great variety of editors will publish your novel, essay or manual (as this one) without any issue.

And don't think on your budget: If you have a good idea, texts, graphics and / or pictures... you can produce really good layouts, through some different applications, all of them free of cost. You do not need a big initial investment, and you will not need to ask for a loan to the nearby bank, in order to have your own books published.

So if you have that idea, this is the right moment to put it into paper (or as an electronic book). Recover those drafts, arrange and complete them. We will see what we can do with them.

Important: this book does not intend to be a compilation of manuals for the different applications proposed to produce a publication. Options are almost infinite. But I want you to have a general view of the whole process... Furthermore, you will find some useful information, such as how to work with the big American editors – or German ones, in Europe. These are growing fast in the last years.

Notes on this edition

This book is the translation of the fourth edition of "**Publicación Online – hazlo tú mismo**", which first was published first in Spanish, on July 2013. In fact, the fourth edition in Spanish to be released in parallel to this one in English.

After the original release, a second edition was needed, since initial feedback from the readers suggested that I should add some more topics. So I used that opportunity to correct some data and to add further information – which resulted in almost twenty pages added to the original version. So a new version was forced (also a new ISBN).

Among the missing topics, I added some hints on text formatting (most important for paperback edition), document export to eBook formats (process that can usually ruin our concept) and the exclusivity on the launch process requested by some major editors.

I also added some reference to the book register process: a legal register of our book is strongly recommended against unwanted copying or plagiarism - this is a personal decision, depending on if your contents are original or adapted, and the final use of the book.

Editors' list was also increased with latest "discoveries" from my side. Most of them small companies, but I also added some missing big ones (for example, you can sell your books through GooglePlay to be read in cell phones and devices with Android)

I also added some minor topic such as the need (or justification) of publishing compilations – for example, from your blog posts. In my opinion, these must be completed, as I will discuss later on, with book-specific contents, so that your readers (probably coming from that blog) will understand the necessity of the publication and thus will purchase it...

As a lesson learned, I redesigned the cover completely (this is also explained in the book). I have to admit that the original design was not really appealing...

Then, third edition added already some feedback from readers and forum participation. For example, it includes the addition of the free tool Sigil for the direct edition of .epub files.

This fourth version (first in English) also includes some data on eBook checking (so that compatibility is assured for most reader devices) and minor edition and correction. Also referencing to Scrivener, a new (paid) way to create books, was added.

Of course, this is a translated book. I hope you will indulge me if I made some big grammatical mistake here... Anyway, I will be glad to receive your constructive feedback on any aspect of this book.

First Steps...

Electronic book or paperback?

Of course, first decision you have to take is if you want to publish an eBook, a paperback or both. You do not need to make all versions at the same time, you may release one first and the other one later on.

The contents in your book may also have some influence in that decision. While a text-only book will publish perfectly on both platforms, we will see that complex layouts (with captions, images, graphics...) may have some problems upon rendering in a portable device.

Anyway, main recommendation is to convert all your documents into a single text document or several ones (maybe per chapters) if the book will be "long".

You will also need digital versions of all images, graphs and pictures that you want to insert in the book, including the cover (we will see that there may be some exceptions to this). For a paperback version, you may want to have high resolution images.

Graphics and Pictures

This is an important point: resolutions used for the publication of an eBook and a paperback are very different, just like the sizes of the generated files. We will see this topic in deep later on.

Usually, if your book will include a big amount of graphic contents, it will look much better in paperback version, with some exceptions (photography books, electronic comic-books...). Anyway, no one will prevent you from publishing on both formats. You should have this clear from the beginning.

Even if the text will be the same for both versions, an (both offline and online) editor will be treat those as different books. So your paperback will most likely include an ISBN, whereas the electronic version might not, or it may have some specific number such as the ASIN from Amazon.

> *Note: In some countries, such as Spain or Germany, ISBN is required for all non-periodic publications.*

Specifically, both numbers may not be identical, since they indicate different products (which will usually have also different prices, and even different distribution channels...).

But, coming back to the images, you have to be sure you can use them in your publication. If you did the photographs, graphics or diagrams you should not worry; if you will use third-party images, you will need to *prove* this right to use them.

In some cases, as in the contents you may find in Wikimedia Commons, images are free to use, as long as you comply with certain restrictions (typically, indicating the author's name and origin of the image).

In some other cases (web images, pictures taken by someone else), it is highly recommended that you get their written approval, as a contract or (at least) per email. This will avoid many later headaches... Even when many "image banks" do provide free content, some conditions may apply for their use in commercial products.

And remember that this also applies to the cover. It would be too sad if your book is removed from the marketplace just because you used an image without the proper rights, wouldn't it?

Needed Hardware

Except for the case where you have some really complicated layout in mind, any personal computer will be enough to edit, lay out and publish your book. Believe me.

You do not need a last-generation Mac computer, not humongous amounts of RAM memory. Of course, the faster your computer is, the better you will work. And, if you will work with many high resolution images, RAM will avoid frequent read / write accesses to your hard drive.

Furthermore, most of the programs described below (mainly the free ones) have versions for all common operating systems, Windows, Mac OS and Linux (Ubuntu and company).

You will just need an Internet connection (or some friend that can download those programs for you, and upload the final book files), and around 500Mb (even up to 1 GB) of free space in your hard drive if you want to install all proposed programs. But I would bet that you have already some of them in your computer...

I would recommend, anyway, a big screen, so you can see the "full" document without zooming out too much – so you can see how the layout looks like from the edition process.

Needed Software

OK then, what programs do you need to dive into the edition world? As you can imagine, this will depend on the kind of publication that you want to do. But, besides, this will also depend on your budget.

Important thing is that your edition or layout Software has "What-you-see-is-what-you-get" (WYSIWYG) capabilities, so that it can show you on screen how the edition outcome will look like and assure that the final result will be just like that, be it either on an eBook reader screen or on paper.

Paid programs

Of course, all major Software providers do have programs for digital contents creation, edition and publication.

Microsoft Word, with more than two decades' history, has evolved to allow for the addition of graphic content and the use of adjustments (line spacing, alignments...), which are becoming more and more professional every day.

In its latest versions, Word allows (at last!) for the direct export to PDF format, which is the most broadly used among print-on-demand (POD) companies. Furthermore, it can also save files as unfiltered HTML, which can be easily converted to electronic books.

For books with mainly text contents, without great layout requirements or graphic content, Microsoft Word can be a good starting point.

For somehow more complex layouts, the company also proposes **Microsoft Publisher,** but this one is nowadays "halfway" from pure text editors to real, professional layout applications (which we will see now). In any case, price is much lower than that of professional layout software.

The company Adobe, on their side, is the de-facto standard for graphic design in general. **Adobe Illustrator** allows for the creation of vector graphics for posters, covers, diagrams, infographics...

Then, **Adobe Photoshop** can be used for the advanced image and photo edition, up to incredible transformations, unthinkable just a few years ago.

To complete the set, **Adobe InDesign** is their tool for professional publication and layout. It is heir to **Aldus Pagemaker** (later on **Adobe Pagemaker**), which was a reference back in the nineties, together with QuarkXpress.

QuarkXpress, from the company Quark, Inc. was the standard software by end of last century. The ease to develop add-ons ("Xtensions") and the possibility of importing almost every file format made QuartkXpress the most powerful layout application of its time.

QuarkXpress also provided multiple professional tools and settings, like pre-press and colour pattern inclusion in the master document.

Scrivener (information manager)

Scrivener is the last addition to the family of programs dedicated to publications creation. In this case, it is an information management software, which allows you to organize all your contents in a visual manner.

Scrivener will let you store "in a same place" all your text documents, images, PDF files... even web pages that you may use as reference and you can export to plain text for later edition. It will also store audio and video files.

Screen captures in the official Scrivener web page

It has a system that mimics the traditional "corkboard", where you may create and pin cards and notes, rearranging them as much as you want.

This way, we can keep track of the characters' profiles in our novel, or define a timeline for our book, arranging the different scenes or chapters.

An interesting point, it allows for the saving of "snapshots" from one project, keeping a copy of all documents, the relationship between them and their position within the global publication.

In a final step, Scrivener will export the final publication to a single text document (DOC), that you may edit on your standard software to apply format and final style.

Free programs

But, with the incredible growth of OpenSource software, many development groups and individual programmers have created multiple programs that can already cover most of the needs of the average user – and some advanced ones.

Besides, the broad developers' community for each of the programs that we will describe now can produce translated versions of the programs (both to languages and computer platforms) almost from the beginning.

If you want to, you may work in your native language throughout the editorial process. Most likely, you might even find some programs translated to local languages or dialects.

And of course you will also find support pages and help forums in those languages. Amount of available resources may change with the specific language, though.

As an added feature, this multilingual development is also available during the use of the programs: you may change the language of menus and tools at any time. This is useful if several people in a team are working in different languages... for example, when producing some manual or book (as this one), you may produce screen captures in the target language.

Let's check some of the most commonly used applications.

Text editors

OpenOffice (which you may download for free from their web www.openoffice.org) appeared as an alternative proposal to Microsoft Office, made by the company Sun Microsystems. It includes a text editor (**Writer**), Spreadsheet calculation (**Calc**), presentations program (**Impress**) and some other basic editors.

Since a few years ago, OpenOffice includes native exporting to PDF, and compatibility with Microsoft file formats is improving day by day.

> **Note**: Paid licenses, such as Microsoft ones are usually different for home or business application, being the main difference the profit obtained by the latter.
>
> If you expect to have some "important" income, you should think of acquiring a license for small company or self-employment... or rather, keep to free Software...

Both visual layout and available tools are very similar to those in the Microsoft suite; the shift from one program to the other should not be a big issue for any user.

Furthermore, the importing of MsWord or MsExcel files into OpenOffice is quite *direct*, maybe with some format loss in case of importing some complex (or new) macro functions, for example.

OpenOffice uses a different file format, ODT (short for Open DocumenT), based in the XML standard. It is compatible with text, spreadsheet, graphics and presentation data.

Of course, to streamline the processes in OpenOffice different file extensions are used, being ODT a generic naming for all of them. Specifically, you may find ".odt" applied in text files, whereas ".ods" will be used for spreadsheets, ".odp" for presentations, ".odg" for graphics...

LibreOffice (www.libreoffice.org) appeared as an alternative (also free) to OpenOffice, from a discussion between a group of developers and Sun Microsystems, leader of OpenOffice.

Starting "core" for LibreOffice was common with OpenOffice, and only the latest versions start to show differences in design and functionality.

LibreOffice is a full office suite, too, and it works also with ODT. It is also compatible with Microsoft files, and it includes native export to PDF, too.

Initially, the selection between OpenOffice and LibreOffice may not be that important. However, it seems that LibreOffice is "better" at keeping the OpenSource philosophy, which is moving the developers towards it. So you should expect more frequent updates and improvement, compared to OpenOffice.

With the application **Writer** (available both in OpenOffice and LibreOffice) you can produce valid text books, including some pictures or graphics, with the usual limitations when publishing in electronics format.

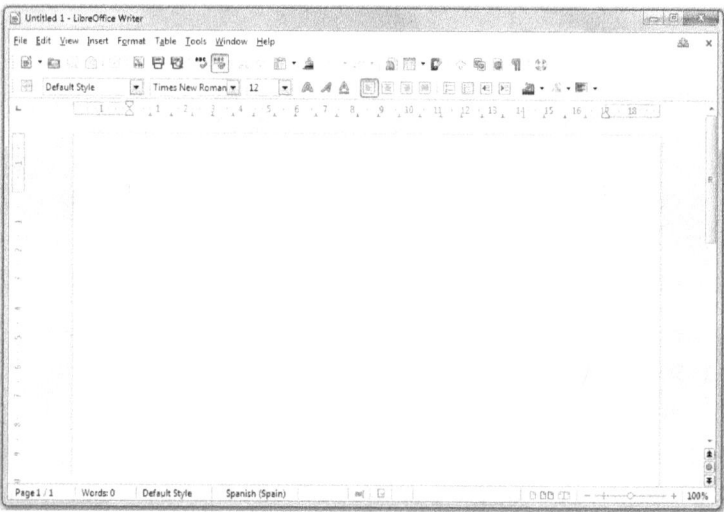

Look of the latest LibreOffice release… icons (and their function) are very similar to those in OpenOffice and the Microsoft suite…

In general, main recommendation will be to import images using the full document width and/or with centre alignment. Images for eBooks will have to be at the same level as text ("anchored") to appear in the final document. Do not insert them as floating elements.

Added to that, some eBook readers are not fully compatible with image captions, so you might consider removing them, explaining the included art in the main text.

Of course, you can (must!) use text editors to prepare your texts if you will work with layout software.

In that case, best practice is to use file formats without any text decoration, such as ".txt", or maybe ".rtf" to include some basic text mark-up (titles, chapters). This way, layout software will not carry over any undesired setting from the original work.

Layout software

Then, regarding layout software, you have also some alternatives to QuarkXpress or Adobe InDesign. The free Software **Scribus** provides many of the standard functions available in the before mentioned, expensive applications.

Working with Scribus will be very similar to any other layout program: creation of "empty" frames for text or image, later selection of the specific content and application of style and decoration.

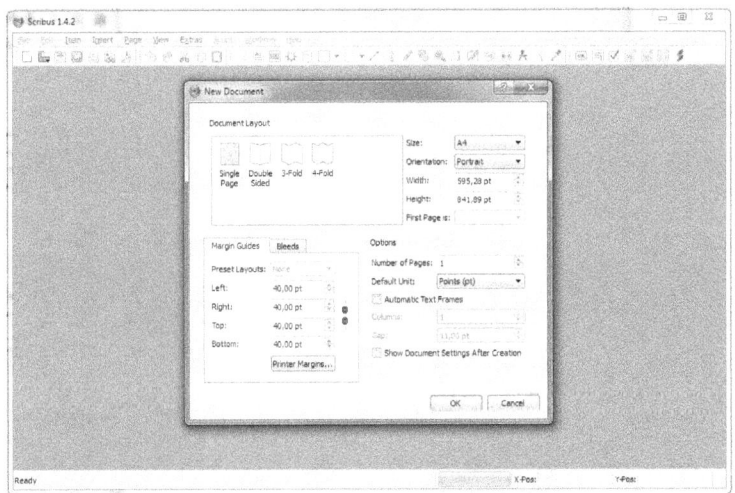

Scribus' start-up screen will help you in the initial document settings configuration…

You have also multiple export options, such as PDF or EPS, including advanced configurations for professional press process.

In the end, this decision is only yours. But if you decide to use free Software such as LibreOffice and Scribus, you might also consider the idea of having all other tools also free. It is really possible to produce professional-looking output, if you work with some discipline, and if you learn to use these tools *the right way...*

> **Note**: *Layout programs allow you to edit texts, in order to apply some correction (or to "paste" partial contents). But you should not use them as "pure" text editors.*
>
> *Included text editors are usually complex to handle, compared to standard text editors.*

Graphics and Photos...

For graphics design and vector graphics, I recommend InkScape (again, free, and available for download at www.inkscape.org). Working process is similar to that of Adobe Illustrator or CorelDraw!

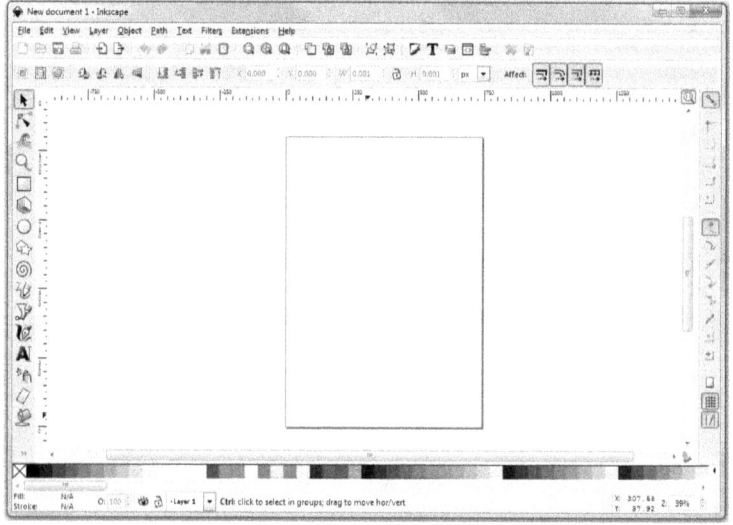

InkScape provides all typical tools in vector graphics applications

InkScape will allow you to draw basic shapes and to produce more complex figures with polygons and curves; you will be able to add texts (to create your covers, for example). InkScape can export to mots "useful" file formats, including JPG, PNG and PDF.

InkScape works also with the OpenSource file format SVG for vector graphics, so that data transfer to other applications is very easy, too.

For photo edition I strongly recommend **GIMP**. You may download it from their web www.gimp.org. It includes a huge variety of functions similar to those in Photoshop and other paid Software (PaitnShop Pro…), but at no cost for you.

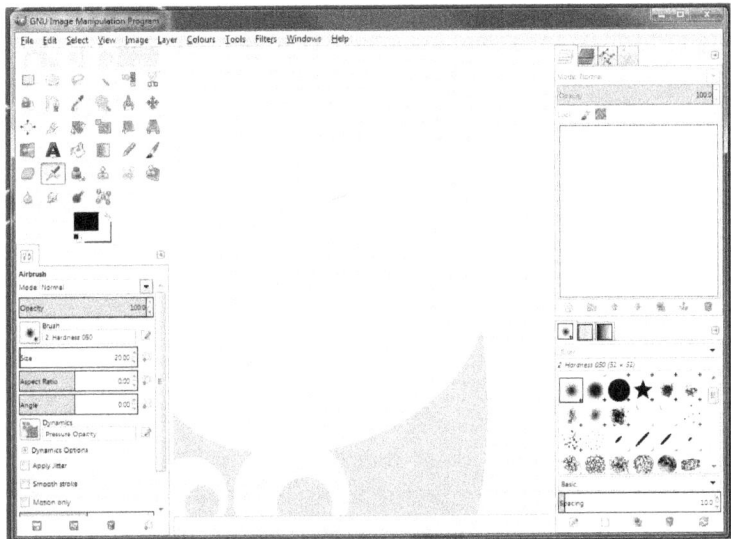

GIMP provides many different edition tools, with similar shortcuts as in Photoshop, including the customization of the tools' windows.

In spite of some current limitations (for example, GIMP will not work with CMYK colour space or with 16-bit-per-channel images), GIMP can cover most of the needs of an advanced user.

Anyway, the different development groups of GIMP are working to improve these (few) weak points day by day, so you should expect to see some improvement in a short time.

If you are used to work with Photoshop, you can also use **GIMPShop**, a GIMP version which mimics the work environment of the Adobe program…

File conversion

Finally, the (also free) application **Calibre** can be used to perform a conversion between the different possible file formats used in eBooks (epub, mobi…), together with the usual DOC, HTML and PDF formats.

This way, you will be able to produce several versions of your eBook, targeting specific reader devices. If you have one specific device, you will be able to work with "native" formats and check the result of your design, or the modifications introduced to a given book.

Calibre allows you to index all your eBooks and to transfer to and from all your devices

> *Note: Are you used to work with some other programs? Use them! The only thing you need is the possibility to export to a valid format or to PDF (for printed books) with some restrictions that we will see later on.*

Sigil: epub editor

But of course, the development community will not stop. Once you have the possibility of creating contents, editing it, preparing a layout, converting it into an eBook… the next logical step is to try and simplify the whole process.

The way to do it is, of course, to create a specific eBook editor, in this case for the broadly used epub file format.

Sigil, available for download from the Google platform at http://code.google.com/p/sigil . Starting with a simple, clean interface, you may directly edit (if you prefer to do so) the HTML / XML information of your eBook.

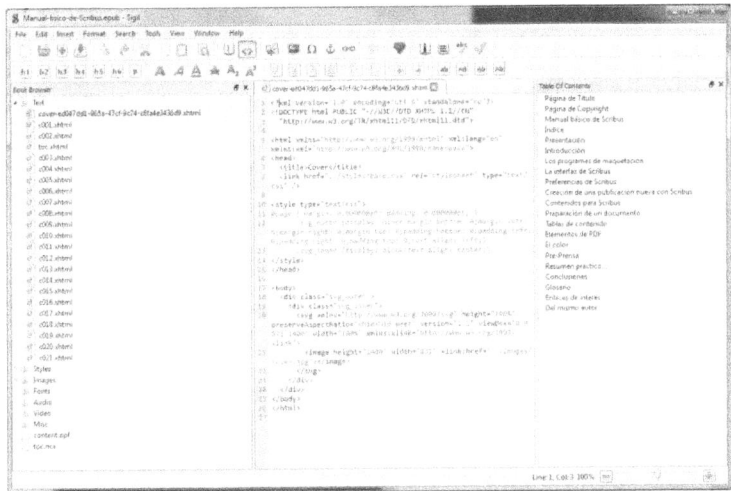

Look of the main edition window in Sigil.

By editing HTML or XML, you may have a full control on the visual finish of your book in eBook readers, even with the possibility of using Cascading Style-Sheets (CSS) or with HTML 5.0 compatible files, readable on any modern web browser (and accepted, for example, by the Amazon import tool).

Other programs

The list of free programs is almost infinite. Depending on the type of contents that you want to publish, you may need certain tools or not.

This would be the case of **RAWTherapee**, one of the best free tools for RAW image edition.

Its interface is different to the usual Windows or Mac OS ones, so the learning curve may be slow. However, it is really a powerful tool.

Advanced image editors, such as RAWTherapee, can show a lot of "hidden", useful data from our images...

Some other programs may help you in "small" things upon completing your book design. Even when applications such as Scribus may generate barcodes (for the ISBN), you can find simpler alternatives.

This is the case of **ZINTPortable** (we will see in a moment the topic of portable applications), which allows for the generation of barcodes for your cover, or even QR-codes (look at the back cover of this book if paperback, or the books listed at the end in the eBook version) for advanced marketing and promotion possibilities.

> *Note: if you want to add a QR-code in your publication to target an Internet address, it is highly recommended to use a generic book page, and not a link to a specific online shop.*
>
> *Doing the latter might create some concerns for other potential distributors of your publication...*

With ZINTPortable you may create your own barcodes and QR-codes...

Portable applications

A very interesting possibility is the installation of programs in an external USB storage media (either flash or hard drive), so that you can use all your applications as "guest" on any computer with the appropriate operating system.

This is the case of the Software available on the Internet site www.portableapps.com, which includes all free tools described so far. Those were modified to allow for an installation without changing the (Windows) registry.

Together with the mentioned applications, there you will find many other different possibilities, from games to system utilities. Then, depending on the capacity of your USB storage, you may include a full working environment in your pocket...

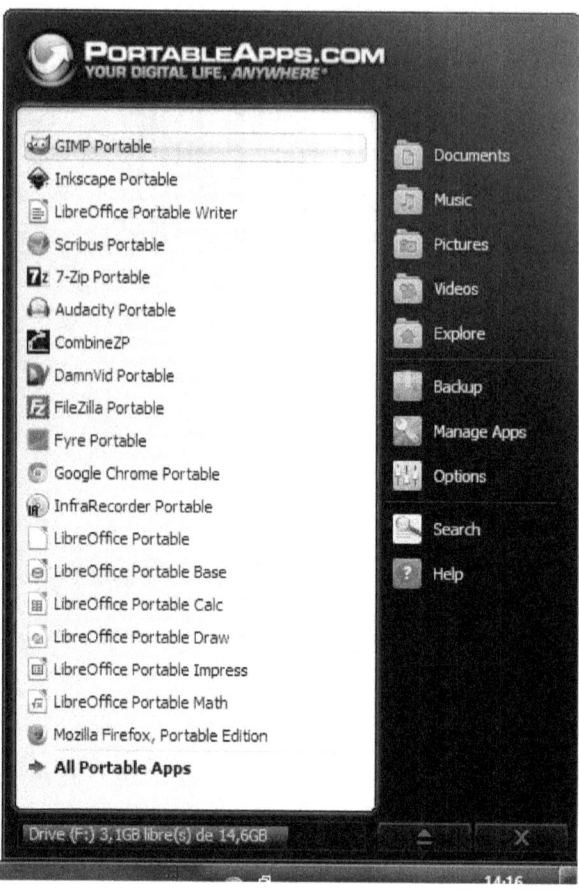

Installation example of the PortableApps platform, with all needed programs for an electronic edition to PDF – all of them free and fully legal...

Structure preparation

Before rushing into "just writing", it may make sense that you prepare an outline of the contents you want to include, so that you may order them and assign priorities, if needed.

This exercise can also help in detecting what would be missing, in case you have already some finished sections for your book.

Check some book on your shelf. Your outline should include some usual sections, depending on the type of book (paper or eBook).

Typically, you will include bibliographic information (title, author, ISBN, copyright...) right after the title page, and you may also want to include some annex at the end, such as a glossary of used terms, information on the characters in your novel, promotion of further books or products...

All these sections will add contents (and pages...) to your publication. From that outline, you will be able to create a preliminary index, and then work on the text and images.

> *Note: If you intend to use "many" texts and images, you might want to create a specific folder to keep your data organized, so that it can be easily recovered later on.*

Texts

It is highly recommended that your text editor includes some kind of language checker and correction tool. Even if your writing is very good, you can always have some typo or use a wrong grammatical expression.

Furthermore, you should use (except in case you are depicting "slang" conversations...) a formal language – and this may not be related to the *seriousness* of the contents, but maybe with the respect towards your readers. Of course, this is a personal decision.

If your book is going to be "long" (a current novel may be between 80,000 and 110,000 words), a good idea is to create separate, maybe numbered, text documents per chapter or section, for example. This will make reviews and later layout much easier, and it may not be needed for simple eBook compositions.

As an added point here, the creation of separate sections in different files can be a good practice, if you intend to write with some collaboration or external reviewers.

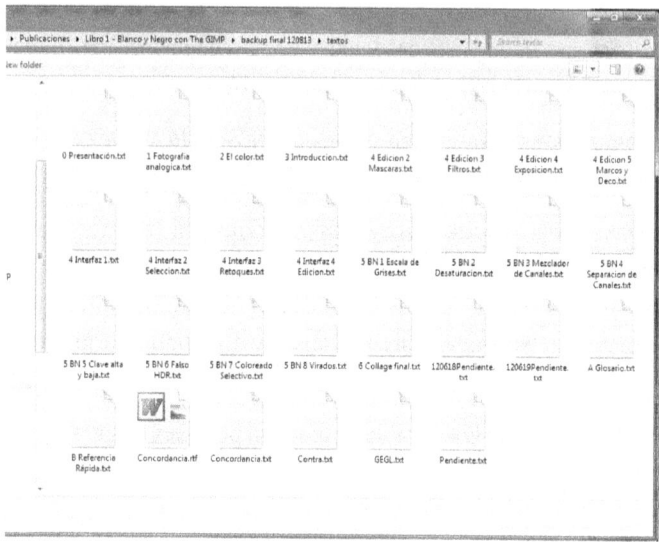

Books with high words-count or many different sections can be easily handled with multiple files...

Regarding file formats, if you are going to work with a layout program, best thing you can do is to use "clean" text formats, such as TXT (plain text).

This will make it easier for those programs to apply the desired fonts and styles, without any unexpected problem. In the layout program you will be able to test different typefaces and style sets, until you find the "perfect" one for your book.

> *Tip*: *If you are preparing a first draft of your book in a plain text editor, label the headers and sub-headers with some special character.*
>
> *Then, upon importing the finished text to your layout software, you will be able to find the separate sections and block easily...*

If you are using text editors (Microsoft Word, OpenOffice / LibreOffice Writer) only, try to stick to the proposed sets of styles (or create a new custom set). Avoid changing manually font, size and decoration, for it will make it much more difficult to update, if you need to make any change.

Anyway, I recommend using the automated header system in your text editor: the different header levels are used by the program later on to create (for example) automated indexes and tables of contents.

Page setting

This is a topic that may drive you crazy in your first editions. Page numbering, for example, is not needed at all. However, it is strongly recommended, since it allows the reader to recall reading at the exact point where he/she stopped, or rather, to find some needed data in a reference or technical book.

And you will find many books (as the paper version of this one) where page numbering does just not start on the first page, but after a certain number of typical contents:

- A page for the title and author
- A page with bibliographical information, including copy rights
- A page with dedication
- One or more pages with quotes or references...

These sections are usually not numbered. Index or Contents table is introduced after those (some authors numbering the pages with roman figures; others prefer to have the index at the end of the book...) and then you may want to add some introduction for the book – even from another person.

Only after all these contents you will place the "real" book contents...

And after the book contents, you may add different annexes, as already indicated. This book, for example, contains a list of terms and acronyms used in the text, a list of useful links and promotion on other books of the author (remember this option for your own marketing strategy).

Some books also include special contents like colour pictures and maps, but this is not so frequent.

In the end, each book will include a number of different sections or chapters. Typically, those are referred to in the header section: this section, for example, is called "First Steps".

To get these header entries with a text editor, you will need to introduce section breaks, so that section headers are independent (not linked to the previous one).

A different case would be if you want to include the title of the book in all sections – in that case, headers must be linked (you can also keep them not linked, then enter the title manually in each section).

You will need to find these options in your specific text editor. Odd and even pages are usually set independently to have, for example, page numbers with different alignment.

Anyway, you will need some practice to master all these settings. My recommendation would be to play with the different options in an empty file – or in a copy of your book: you don't want to ruin the text…

In layout programs, situation is slightly different, with some more options available. You might even create new master pages (both left and right) for each section, with different layout, styles… and contents.

Variations at publishing

Sometimes, it is "allowed" to reuse previous contents as the starting point for a new book. If you are the author of those previous contents, you will not find any issue, here.

If the contents are adapted from other third party work, you will usually need to quote it and obtain, in advance, an authorization for the use of those contents, in much the same way as already indicated for images in previous sections.

This said, there are several different ways that you can reuse your previous work into new books. Let us check some of those.

Compilations

You may have a successful blog, or you published a series of articles or short stories in webs or paper magazines. Great! A good idea can be to publish a compilation of these articles (or the best ones...), to offer them as a whole.

However, you must take care of some issues, when creating such compilations.

For example, if you have a devoted public, always expecting something new from your side, they might not welcome just a listing of previous publications. They might expect some introduction or justification for the new book, or maybe some "guiding" indications that show continuity between posts, as you put them in some logical order.

You may also add some new contents, to complement or complete your original work. Bear in mind again that your readers may need a justification to buy your book.

Of course, if you are very prolific at writing, you may extend your publication to several books, too. Currently there is a trend of publishing (and filming) trilogies – as it seems, you cannot close a story in only one book.

In case you are indeed planning to publish several books with a common line, you will also have to take further decisions, such as the way that you will be releasing the different books:

- You may choose to publish all of them with a short time between one and the following one, which can be used to tease your readers with a first, engaging, low-priced book, so that they will buy the regularly-priced following books.
- Alternatively, you may opt for the planned publication at some "given" dates, so that your public can know when to expect a new release from your side.

The decision on which way to go will depend on the kind of promotion you want to do, and the expected *behaviour* from your side: some readers will want frequent updates, whereas some others may read you only during vacation.

If you decide to act as editor, compiling works from different authors, all of the above applies, too. You should look for a common line to introduce the different parts to the reader in a logic, sequential reading. Remember, a book is not a website anymore, where you may jump from one end to the other.

Re-editions

Another usual practice is (as in the case of the Spanish version of this book) to re-edit previous books.

As I commented in previous sections, printing on demand does not need to produce huge batches of books; there is no stock issue anymore. You will not have a heap of old books laying around and you will not need to plan the new batch in advance.

However, you may want to update the contents, adding or deleting some parts, maybe even changing the order of your sections, in order to make it nicer to your readers.

In most cases, you will need to go through the whole edition process that we will explain shortly, as if it was a brand new book. Of course, you can reuse the previous valid texts and images from the previous edition.

But surely you will find that you introduced too many important changes (well, this is what justifies a new edition...), even your page count may have increased.

For any editor or printer, this will mean a completely new product, with its own reference number, or ISBN (we will see the ISBN in a next section).

For you, this can mean to have two different books on sale at the same time, if you want to. You may lower the price of the previous version, or rather remove it from the market completely. Once again, it is your decision.

Book versions

A last, interesting option can be the creation of different versions of a same book.

For example, you may launch a small-sized version (the paperback version of this book is 5 by 8 inches), and another bigger version, maybe with added notes, unabridged texts or premium content.

Many offset printers do a first book release in large format and then produce a pocket version some time later. This is a traditional marketing strategy, which suggests that some customers are willing to pay a bit more to have a product "as soon as possible". The manufacturer produces accordingly a better product in terms of quality and finish; in our case this might mean a hard cover version with sleeve, for example.

Then, the smaller, cheaper version is released once the sales of the premium product start to drop, to cover the demand of a second group of clients who prefer to wait and buy at a better price.

You might even go for the edition of a full-colour book and one black and white version. Typically, colour printing in POD systems is much more expensive and then selling prices need to be higher, too. In this case, the reader can decide whether to pay the premium price or not, to get the "original" colour contents.

In all cases, every different version that you may produce will be a different book for your editor, and it will have its own ISBN. This can provide you a better visibility on Internet shops, since you will have "more books" published.

But pay attention, this can also confuse your readers, if the offer is just too wide for a single book. If you decide to publish different versions of a book, make sure the differences are clear to the customer.

Of course, translations of your book to other languages make very nice added versions to your portfolio.

Things to do and things to avoid

When you are editing your book, you have to consider certain aspects that will make your book nicer to read. This will improve your reader's experience. For example, you might want to check the following:

- Spelling and grammar. Please. Poorly-written books will create a very bad image of you, which might lead to sell misses.
- For an eBook, you must remove all headers and footers. Most electronic readers will render those wrong. Notice that the reader may change the type size and then page "ending" cannot be fixed.
- Same thing as above for text footers and notes...

- You must avoid multiple new line returns. This will also render horribly in an eBook reader. Instead, use the line spacing options of your editor or layout program.
- Use a finite set of fonts and styles. You may choose the preconfigured sets in your editor, or create a new set. This will allow you for later changes in the text appearance in a single step.

In the following sections, I will review the creation of electronic books. Until then, please keep the above recommendations at hand.

Style guidelines

An interesting piece of advice, you might want to create your own style guidelines. Depending on the kind of publication, this may not be needed, but it is always good to have this list visible when checking of your publication.

For example, you may decide that all words and terms in a foreign language are shown in *italics,* to indicate that "something is happening here".

Or rather, you may remove (as I was suggested from a previous version of this book) all suspension points at the end of the paragraphs.

If your book includes dialogs, you should define the type of language to be used by your characters, fillers, common expressions or special vocabulary.

And even if your book does not include dialogs you will have to define the general *tone* of your book, if it will be formal or more colloquial, even allowing for some informal expressions and slang. You have to decide who is your target reader, so that you adapt your writing style and make the text nicer to read.

Having all sections a common fonts set (I will repeat this several times throughout the book) helps also to make reading a comfortable experience, mainly in printed versions. This is important if you will create your publication from different documents or sources. Slight changes in type faces and sizes will provide a "strange feeling" to the reader, even if the change is not clearly visible.

In a similar way, you may want all your chapters to begin in an odd page (right side, you may need to add a blank page). In this case, you will check that no chapter starts in an even page (left) to produce a solid publication. Obviously, this point is not critical for eBooks.

If you check on the web pages of the editors listed in late sections, you may find that most of them provide already a valid styles guidelines document. In most cases, those are just recommendations "that work", and it is worth checking them to begin with.

Of course, you do not need to follow all rules and guidelines. You may want to break some of them to add your own personality to your publications, in a way that will make you stand out from other authors.

Images

If you are going to include images in your publication, you should also compile them (as already indicated before) in a known, dedicated folder, so that you may recall them easily later on to be included in your book.

A good practice may be the renaming with key words o section names, so they will be easily found: it is quite common to end up with a folder full with "DSCF" or "IMG" files...

Anyway, there are two parameters that you need to check for all your images: colour space and resolution.

Colour space

Usually, you will work with images in RGB mode, with 24 bits per pixel resolution. Even if you are working with black and white images, or with indexed colour, it is better to convert them to RGB to avoid any compatibility issue upon exporting to PDF.

As an added feature, your image editor may give you the option to store your images as sRGB or AdobeRGB. Both options refer to enhancements of the original RGB space definition, optimizing the coverage in output colours. But you do not need to know about all these technical things. If possible, use AdobeRGB (and not sRGB). If you do not have this option, just save as plain RGB and don't worry any more.

> *Note: You may also work in "native" CMYK mode, which (in theory) will improve colour compatibility – or colour matching – with your printing company.*
>
> *However, this will mean a higher amount of data, so your files may get bigger, and your computer could work slowly... just to get some slight improvement in the output, usually negligible.*

And, again, this applies also to black and white. Here you have two options: to convert all your images to (Adobe) RGB, or rather to greyscale, which can provide some added flexibility to the press company in order to use plain black ink...

Resolution

You will produce your books to be read at short distances, maybe at a maximum half a meter. If you want to include a high level of detail (for example, some graph with values on the axes), you will need to use a high resolution.

Electronic devices have usually a limited resolution, ranging from the 72ppp in old monitors to the current 266ppp in the "Retina" panels by Apple and some other manufacturers.

If you include high-resolution images in an electronic book, these may not render well in the eBook reader, or the device will have to downscale it (with some quality loss) to fit it in the display.

In any of both cases you will not use the high-resolution. You will just create a big eBook file.

So in order to publish in electronic format you should target images around 800 x 600 (small 6in. e-Ink displays) or maybe 1024 x 768 pixels.

Anyway, you should check updated product releases – HD screens with 1920 x 1080 pixels are a current trend... then, maybe 2Mp should be the target for your embedded images. Also notice that these displays are not pure e-Ink displays, but usually LCD or IPS panels.

> *Note: this could be a practical limit to your images – around 2Mp. Do not try to include your 16Mp photos in an eBook...*

On the contrary, industrial presses work typically with resolutions above 300ppp (quite often, around 600ppp).

Depending on the physical dimensions of the book (format, bind) and the needed margins and gutter, you will be able to calculate the needed "minimum" dimensions for your images. Calculations are identical to those to produce paper prints of your pictures.

> *Example*: *a 4" x 6" picture, printed with 300ppp resolution, "needs" 1,200 x 1,800 pixels, around 2Mp…*

Again, a book with many high-resolution images will use a lot of memory in your computer, both for the final document and in the working RAM memory as you edit it. If your computer is not very powerful, you should expect a slow process.

The cover

Most online editors will request a separate document (either PDF or JPG) for the cover, since it will have a fixed format or form factor (in case of paper printing, the cover should include at least the spine and back cover).

Depending on the design that you are considering, you will be able to do it with your layout program (Scribus, InDesign), with your vector graphics tool (InkScape, Illustrator) or rather with your image editor (GIMP, Photoshop). Main requirement is that it should allow for the exporting to PDF, if needed.

For formal documents (projects, essays, thesis), a cover prepared in your word processor may be enough, too.

For standard paperback editions, each editor may request specific conditions. If your cover has a background or main image, which should end with the cover border, you may be requested to send a slightly bigger image (say, five millimetres) to allow for easier manufacturing and to avoid white lines upon book trimming.

This "lost" section is called *bleed* in the technical environment.

> *Note*: *For some editors such as CreateSpace, spine design is critical. With 100 pages or less, text should be just too small, so you may not be able to use it properly.*

In a similar way, all images in the book interior that must reach the page border will be requested to have some bleed, to ensure a perfect result.

And this is the reason why many editors try also to avoid any kind of content in the margins areas. Page numbers, headers and footers must lay within a safety limit, which can vary from scarce ten millimetres to more than twenty in the gutter, if your book has a lot of pages. This will facilitate reading, but also binding and trimming.

Finally, for paperback publications a space is reserved (typically in the back cover) for the introduction of the ISBN barcode.

Image sources for your cover

The cover of a book is, in most occasions, your visit card to sell a book. A bad cover can cause rejection or lack of interest in your potential readers. And I know it, you can believe me.

Ideally, book title should be readable even for miniatures, so that it can be read in the listing of your favourite online shop. If your readers cannot find your book at a glance, you are already missing some chances from the beginning.

And, together with the title, you need to produce an appealing cover. You will add a main image, or create a full cover design. You have to be outstanding from your competitors.

So one of the main tasks upon cover preparation can be the search of a valid, impacting image.

Fortunately, there are several ways to get images. If you like photography (and/or image edition) and are good at it, you can capture or create your own images.

Alternatively, you can access online *image banks,* which offer incredible amounts of photos and graphics to choose from, either free or at a reasonable low cost.

> **Note**: *You must read the small print. Some of these webs put some limits or conditions for image use, if it will be inserted in commercial products.*

Of course, you can always access Wikimedia Commons (you can find it at http://commons.wikimedia.org/), a reference web for multimedia source. Most images include a copyright description, with the conditions for use (most times, you just have to name the source). But you will find many other webs worth checking, such as the following ones:

- **Flickr**: they have a section (free stock) of free images.
- **USA Government**: Interesting site with scientific and historic images, most of them free to use.
- **Freeartisticphotos.com**, they will request attribution of the image, you would need to contact them in advance.
- **4freephotos.com,** a huge collection of images free for commercial use, with attribution needed.
- **Goodfreephotos.com,** several thousands of public domain images.
- **PublicDomainFiles.com,** including not only photos but also graphics, fonts and video clips.
- **Photos-public-domain.com,** explicitly allowing for commercial use, except when indicated.
- **Freestockphotos.biz,** around 14,000 images with different use licenses available.
- …

The ISBN

ISBN is the short for International Standard Book Number. It is a unique identifier for each publication, whatever its type: book, magazine...

ISBN-10 structure. Source: Sakurambo at English Wikipedia / WikiMedi Commons

It consists of ten or thirteen digits, which indicate the editor, title, country or countries of publication (for example, to provide information on the language)... The system is quite complex, I can recommend you to check the Wikipedia entry on ISBN.

> *Note*: *One ISBN refers to one specific publishing process, so that number of pages and format are frozen.*
>
> *If you need to change those (after a first edition) you will have to use a new ISBN and release.*

Anyway, you need to know that ISBN may not be needed (in some specific countries, such as Spain or Germany, it is compulsory if you want to have a commercial distribution).

ISBN barcode has become a usual part of most book covers.

However, most book shops and libraries worldwide use it, so if you plan to have your books in those channels you should consider seriously the need of using the ISBN. And here you will have to take some first decisions:

- **You can get an own ISBN,** so that you register as book editor. You have all rights, and you may contract any printing company to produce your book.

  Since this is penalizing the printer (the book does not belong to them, commissions are different), external editors or printers usually charge you (at least as an initial payment) "for the inconvenience", typically around 100 – 150€

  Positive point is that you may print wherever you want, even at several editors / printers simultaneously.

  Each country usually has its own ISBN agency, connected to the main offices in the United States. Prices vary a lot from single-ISBN purchases to wholesale batches.

- **You may request the editor to get the ISBN for you**, so that you still keep all rights, but the ISBN already refers to the specific editor.

Usually, you will be charged some processing fee, lower than the previous one. Your ISBN will only be valid for that specific editor. If you want to go to another one, you will need to request a new ISBN.

- **You may leave all paperwork to the editor**, and in this case they own the rights *to publish* (pay attention: you always have the rights on the contents). Again, the ISBN will include a reference to the editor, so that you will not be able to use it somewhere else.

Typically, you will not be charged with this option, but you can always find some "pirate" company that will try to get as much money from you as possible...

As a reference, ISBNs cost just a few cents, when bought in batches of several thousands.

In the description of the editorial process, I will indicate when we have to request the ISBN.

> *Note: as indicated, ISBN includes a reference to the number of pages; if you make some change to the book that affects this number, you will need to make a new ISBN request.*

Except in case you plan to be an editor yourself, all three options are very similar. You will have to decide which one suits you best for each specific publication.

> *Tip: Most POD editors allow you to remove a book from their lists. You may publish with a free editor's ISBN and then re-edit with your own ISBN, if you foresee a big success.*
>
> *You might need to do it as a second edition, or you may add a new introduction, some extra contents...*

...and other numbers

Some companies try to avoid internal stock management through ISBNs. There are a lot of alternative codes, depending on the company or institution.

For example, Amazon uses its own coding, the ASIN (Amazon Standard Identification Number) for all its products online, both physical and electronic.

In general, you will find anything, from library-specific codes (CODEN, ISSN...), for music (ISMN) or even... for German books published in the 16th century (VD16)...

Creation of an eBook

It is not my intention to teach you how to write. I am sure you can do much better than me. If you are considering the publication of your work, that part should already be solved...

Anyway, it is always good to read about the topic (you have to always try and improve...), to learn how other (successful) writers work, how to define your own style, how to adapt your language to the kind of book or target reader... A few basics can improve you books' quality spectacularly.

From that point on, the creation of an electronic book can be very simple, but you might as well want to understand how eBook readers work when reading your files...

Function of an eBook reader

EBook readers are just XML document viewers or renderers. They allow the user to specify font size (sometimes, font face, too), together with margins and line spacing.

This way, each reader will "see" a different eBook. You may not fix any of these parameters – thus the need to store the file in specific formats, such as *unfiltered* HTML (a type of simple XML document).

This way, most eBook readers are somehow limited when rendering variable line spacing, indents, tabs... so main advice here is to keep to plain text, maybe **bold** and *cursive,* headings defined with HTML tags (or with your text editor' styles).

But main limitation of these devices (also an advantage, in terms of battery life!) is the use of e-Ink (electronic ink) panels, which render the texts and images without any flicker or refresh, so that the eye is not stressed.

As negative point, current e-Ink technologies only allow for the definition of sixteen different grey shades, including white and black, so that images may not show properly.

You should also minimize the use of tables and lists (both ordered and unordered), even when lists might render right in some readers. Most likely, indents and line spacing will ruin the list...

Electronic ink

Main difference between the screen in a tablet and the one in an eBook reader is the technology used. Electronic "ink" is stored in small capsules all over the screen surface. Black and white pigments are moved closer or farther from the surface by means of the application of an electrostatic charge.

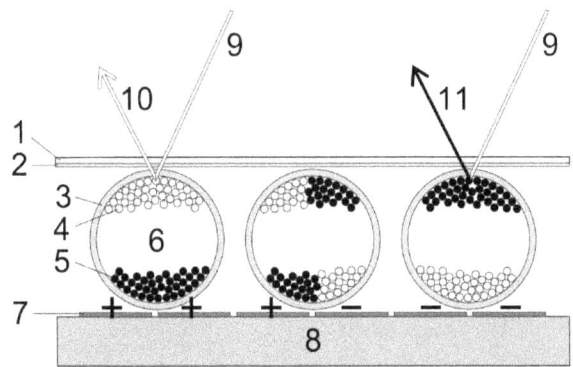

1. Top layer
2. transparent electrode
3. transparent micro-capsules
4. White pigments, positive charged
5. Black pigments, negative charged
6. Transparent oil
7. Electrodes / pixels layer
8. Support / Substrate
9. Light
10. White
11. Black

Structure of electronic paper (side view of an electrophoretic screen). Source: Tosaka for WikiMedia Comons, based on Ref:NIKKEI ELECTRONICS 2008.12.29 Issue Page.69

If the black pigment is in the outer position, black will be visible. In the most inner position, it will not be visible, and then white will be seen on the screen. Between these two cases, another 14 statuses are possible, related to intermediate grey shades. To distinguish between the 16 shades, only ambient light is needed.

Tablets, on their side, use LCD technology, with a higher number of different colours' rendering possible (typically, 65,000). They need back illumination, so that thicknesses are usually bigger, and battery consumption is also higher.

> *Note: some initiatives, like the colour e-Ink screens from Qualcomm, did not do it to the market due to different issues…*

As a response to the increasing tablets market, latest eBook readers are already including backlight as an added feature, in order to read in low ambient light conditions.

Document preparation

OK, so you have your book, your images, and you want to produce your electronic book. Quite easy. We will use first a text editor. You just need to follow some basic rules (some of which were already described in previous sections):

- Order your texts (if you have separate files) in a single document, and remove all text decoration (if these are not matching between sections)
- Mark your headers and sub-headers (up to a fourth level, at most) with the integrated buttons or shortcuts in your editor
- For an eBook, remove all footer (including page numbering), header and notes information.
- Insert your images with the command "Insert – Image – From File…" (This may vary with your editor). Use a new line for each image, without text. Remember to use a maximum image size as for your target eBook reader screen.
- Go through your text, in case you need to apply some specific decoration (bold, cursive…). Run the spell-check again. Yes, once more, please.
- Remove all duplicated new lines; if you do not do it yet, you should get used to applying line spacing only…

- Introduce page breaks at every new chapter (Usually through the use of "Ctrl + Enter"), so that every new chapter will start in a new page.
- Add the bibliographic information:
    - First page must contain only the tile and author(s) name.
    - Second page (with page break) will also include ISBN, copyright data... here you may also add version or edition number
    - Third page will contain dedications or quotes...
- Once all the above is done, you may create the index or table of contents, which will link to your chapter headers. You will find some option like "Insert table of contents" or "Indexes and References"... Make sure you uncheck the box related to the inclusion of page numbers (these will change in the device depending on the selected type size).
- Export or save your document, for example as unfiltered HTML file. Your text editor will generate a document similar to a web page, together with a folder containing all used images.

At this point you would already have a document "visible" in some eBook devices. If your device can render these HTML files, make sure you also copy the images to the indicated folder, so that the reader can find them and show them in the right place inside your text.

However, some editors will just not accept the HTML with the linked images. Amazon, for example, requests all data to be sent in a ZIP container. Other editors may request specific epub or mobi files to be uploaded.

Fonts...

An interesting topic, usually not considered in first publications, is the set of font styles to be used in a book.

If you make a quick search on Internet, you will find a lot of pages speaking about readability and ergonomics. There is some difference between typefaces with and without serif (decoration) and indications on when you should use an indent or an extra line spacing to begin a new paragraph. In general, you should NOT do both in a same text...

> *Note: For example, the paper version of this book is edited with a font face without serif (Calibri) and paragraphs start with increased line spacing.*

Line spacing will be related to the font size and the desired readability for your text. This way, for only-text books such as novels or essays, line spacing is equal to the character height.

Official or legal texts will increase this spacing, maybe to twice or three times the character height. In between, your text editor will allow you to select some intermediate values, like 1.15, 1.25, 1.5... times the character height.

Layout programs such as InDesign and Scribus let you go one step further, and you may define exact line spacing in terms of points and picas (units used in professional press).

Anyway, your first decision must be the font size. In an eBook this is not so critical, since the device will adjust that size to the user setting. However, when printing in paper, this can be a value to investigate in deep...

The paper version of this book uses a 9pt font size and 1.15 line spacing. A bigger font size would have produced just too few words per line, and few lines per page.

Bigger books may allow you to use bigger font sizes, so that they can be read from a longer distance. However, you should not exaggerate when setting your base size – your book might look "empty" if you set a too big font size or large line spacing.

Decoration

Most edition programs will allow you to add some decoration effect to your fonts, such as "drop caps", that can produce a bigger first letter (or first word) in a new paragraph. Size of this bigger font is typically three to five lines:

This way, you may highlight the beginning of a new chapter, for example (of course, you should not use this effect on all paragraphs: the effect would not look good...).

You may probably need to do some printing test (with your home printer) to see the preliminary effect of your font selection and line spacing setting, until you find the right combination…

> *Note*: *Again, layout programs will give you more freedom upon fixing the desired values. You should be able to define all character parameters for your book, then change it to optimize your layout "on the fly"…*
>
> *You can even define your font size with decimal places to get the perfect fit of your text in the text areas…*

The cover…

As already commented, the capabilities of the eBook devices' screens are quite limited.

So you do not need to produce a very high-resolution image. However, it can be as complex as you want it to be. Only the final file format should be usually JPG or PDF.

Again, you should work in a most generic way. So when you are done with your image, remember to store it in RGB space (or AdobeRGB) if you were not using it already. A size around 1024 x 768 (or 800 x 600) can be enough (check the requirements of the online editor). It would produce files around 200Kb in JPG with high quality setting (low compression).

A full cover (including back cover and spine) can include many different elements…

Use of Calibre

In a previous section I spoke of the need of converting a DOC file into HTML, epub or mobi file formats. And, of course, we do have a tool to do it, Calibre.

The way to work with Calibre will be to "import" the source file (DOC, HTML, PDF, epub…) to our library and to select the output file format. We can upload it directly to the eBook reader (connected via USB, WiFi…), to check the introduced changes.

Calibre also allows you to insert the cover image in the eBook document, just by selecting it from the computer. In this case, only the front cover is usually inserted.

Anyway, some editors (such as Amazon) may still request to have the cover in a separate file, it will also be used in their online shop and promotions.

> *Tip*: create a folder to store all generated eBooks, maybe with the date or number in the file name. This will help you in tracking version changes…

The specific online editor may request also a PDF file, or rather the epub version. Or maybe a ZIP with the unfiltered HMTL and all images…

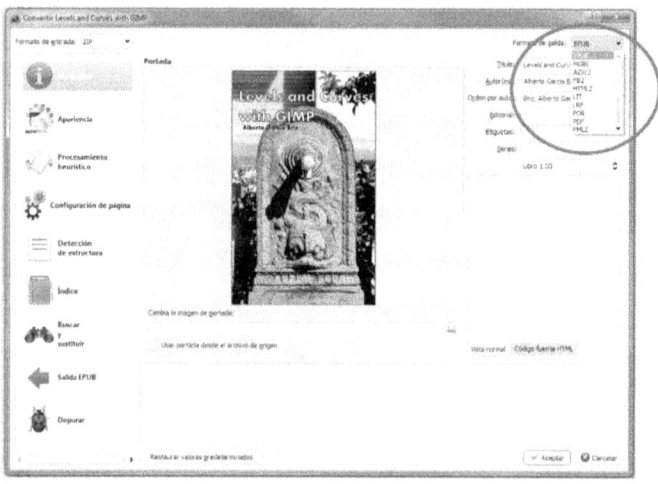

Calibre can generate electronic books in multiple file formats…

Creation of a paper book

In case you want to publish a paper book, preparation of the contents is quite similar. However, we have some added topics to worry about, if you want a quality product.

Book format

First important decision is the size of your book. Most online editors will provide several size options (big, around "Letter" size, or rather small, pocket ones) and form factors (landscape, portrait or square).

Even when POD companies have some freedom when printing with special sizes, you may find that your favourite bookstore does not accept certain dimensions, usually because of logistic constraints: maybe the size of their shelves in the storage area is not matching that of your book...

> **Note**: the paper version of this book was produced in a 5" x 8" size (around 127 x 203 millimetres)

So recommendation is to work with standard formats, if you don't need some critical dimension due to a design decision...

Book size and form factor will define (together with the font size) some other critical aspects in your book. In case of this book, the number of pages forced a "thin" spine, so CreateSpace did not allow for the introduction of text on it...

Colour or Black and White?

Next decision will be if you just need black ink (usual for text-only books, essays, novels), or maybe full colour printing. One single colour image makes your book a colour one. If you want to add one colour (for example, blue headers..., this will also make a colour POD print, since it has to be produced in a CMYK system.

> **Note**: Some modern POD editors, such as BoD (Books on Demand) will allow you to mix black and white pages with colour ones, so that the final price is not jeopardized by a few illustrations.

And the request to use colour implies the use of white paper, to assure proper colour rendering. This could also reduce the creative possibilities of your book.

If you use only black ink, some editors will offer cream coloured paper, maybe nicer to the eye...

> *Example*: this book includes some colour pictures and screen captures. However, black and white printing was chosen for the paperback version, in order to keep production costs within acceptable limits...

An important point here, you might want to check a printed proof of your book before publishing it.

This can help you in detecting some printing issues. First edition of this book included the notes (as the above ones) in a lighter grey shade. Since the printer process used by CreateSpace has a (relatively) low resolution, you could see the black dots pattern used to create the light grey, which affected the rendering of these texts and greyscale screen captures.

Anyway, you can always have some bad results. You may get a valid proof from one printer company (say, in the US), then get some purchased sample out of a European facility with a different appearance... POD companies cannot assure 100% identical results from different facilities.

Bleed, margins

That should be your next decision. You have to indicate if the contents in your book will reach the page border (the named "bleed") or not. If you have a single page in these conditions, you will need to declare your *full book* as with bleed.

This has some impact in the manufacturing process of the book, specifically on the preparation of the different master sheets.

This way, for a given book size, they will be able to fit more or less pages in a single master sheet, which can have an impact in the manufacturing costs of your book.

> **Note**: *Most online editors have an online calculator for book costs and pricing, so that you may have a first approach, in advance, of your book's costs.*
>
> *Use that calculator to detect if there is some specific parameter that can be penalizing your book...*

But you may just find that this is not your case. Some presses (also traditional ones) already include marks and symbols outside the pages (for aligning, colour check...), so main sheet usage is anyway limited.

Traditional presses used these marks to assure the alignment among the different colours upon printing (colours were printed separately), and also for the final binding and cutting processes.

In POD printing, colour alignment is not needed, since printing is done in a single pass.

Resolution, colour space, image formats...

As already indicated, images for a paper publication should be in high-resolution. If this is not so, you may find two different types of issues in the final print:

- **The image shows blurry contours, lack of focus:** typically, the image was enlarged with an image editor, applying a low-pass filter (blur) to avoid possible aliasing.

- **The image shows aliasing and noisy structures:** If an image is enlarged without the application of low-pass filters, all defects and artefacts will be more visible.

Usually we will not be able to control the effect of enlargement, so we will have one of the two situations above.

In a best case, we will be able to control the compression level of the JPG format, which should be set to low (low compression, high quality) to avoid highlighting the above described problems.

JPG, PNG, TIF

Of course, the way to avoid those problems is to use high quality images throughout the process, with a minimum 300ppp (being 200ppp the very practical limit), storing in low-compression JPG, or rather as PNG or TIF formats.

And remember to use the colour space Adobe RGB on all images, when available.

Depending on how you work with your text editor or layout program (if you insert, or copy-paste, or link the images), you may want to store all images in a same folder, as proposed in previous sections.

Contents distribution, layout, book style

Distribution of your contents in the book will be the key step in your publication. You will need to have a clear idea on how every page *type* should look like.

Even if your book is a novel, left and right pages design may be different. Margins may be different on the sides, page numbers are placed on the outer side, and you may want to add (as in this book) different headers for the book title, section or chapter.

Once you know how your pages will look like (a good idea could be to draw them in a piece of paper as a reference), you will need to adapt the master pages, creating as many as you need to facilitate your work flow.

> **Note**: *The use of master pages is only needed if you are planning complex compositions, and only when you work with layout programs...*

After the master pages definition, you will also check the fonts styles set and create a new one, if you want to. You may define specific font faces, decoration, line spacing... for all different types of texts (plain, header, image caption...).

As already indicated, with layout programs you will have many more configuration options and possibilities than with your standard text editor – or at least these options will be more accessible.

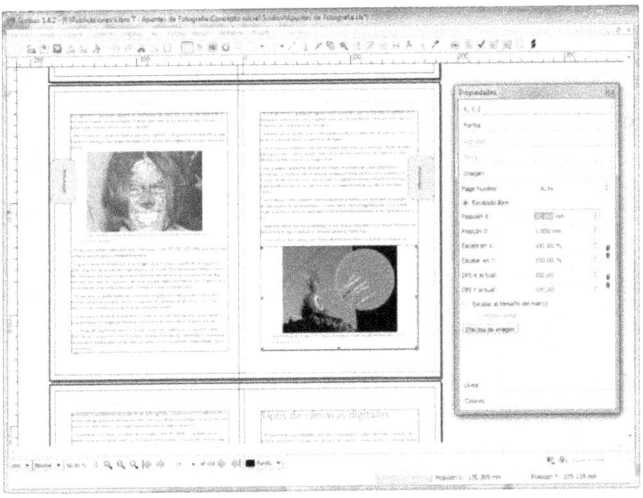

Workspace in Scribus is a bit more complex than that of text editors...

Layout process will be similar in all programs: first you need to define "empty" boxes or containers, then you indicate which text or image goes in, by selecting the appropriate TXT, DOC or JPG document.

All layout programs let you link different text (even different size, and in different pages...) boxes in a series, so that long texts will flow continuously through them. This can even be done when pages are not sequential (you may have, for example, a full-page image, a table or a graph, then the text will skip that page)

You can also overlay different objects (images, text and decoration) to produce the desired composition.

Once the layout is finished, editors will let you make a check on the document, in order to detect major or minor issues. This verification will check different topics, depending on the target document format (PDF, EPS...)

Layout programs can detect, for example, if there is a text "overflow" (a long text cannot be fully inserted in the selected frame or frames). Then, you may need to increase the frame size, or rather link the frame to a next one.

Also images with low resolution (which would result in poor quality) can be detected. And they can also find linked images with missing reference file…

Export

Once the layout is finished and corrected, you may create a first PDF file, which should contain all elements in the same layer. Some online editors may request you to remove all transparency, which can be important when defining the layout concept and colour palettes.

Since you will be sending the PDF file to a professional service, you should select the latest standard format available (for example, PDF version 1.5) and, if you have the option, set image resolution to at least 300ppp. This will ensure the compatibility of your system with the press one.

When you work with high-resolution, high-quality images, you should expect big file sizes. 150Mb – 200Mb can be easily obtained, if you include many images in your book…

But don't worry. All online editors have upload systems based on FTP protocol, so the process will not last that long.

Cover

You may edit your cover, again, with your favourite application, depending on the design that you look for (just text, simple graphics or full page photography…). You may also want to add some logo, and the ISBN barcode (some online editors will add it for you and then you just need to leave the blank space).

Anyway, the process is similar, and you should end up with an image with high resolution (the previous 1024 x 768 would not be right anymore), maybe as PDF file. Then, cover document may also be a big file…

> *Example*: The cover of the paperback version of this book, done on 5" x 8", needs a minimum 1,500 by 2,400 pixels (around 3,6Mp), if we intend to print with 300ppp resolution. In JPG format, this may mean around 1Mb file…
>
> And if you do a full cover (including spine and back cover) the quantities double…

If you want to use a full image for your cover, remember to add the bleed dimensions (so the image must be bigger), to allow for slight deviation sin the printing / trimming process, avoiding unwanted white border lines.

Some editors will provide online cover creation tools, so that cover creation is made simpler – but at a cost, you will only have a few cover templates available.

Alternatively, you may download cover templates (in PDF, PNG or SVG formats) that you may later edit with your favourite program, be it an image editor (such as GIMP or Photoshop) or a vector graphics program (InkScape, Illustrator).

When designing your cover, please consider your target reader. One of the lessons learned from the first edition of this book is that the cover must be appealing to your public, and follow current styling trends.

Here you can compare the original cover (in the Spanish version) with the cover for the second edition – these are two very different concepts...

Together with the contents, you must find the right cover for your publication...

As you can see, those are two different books... Second design pretended to attract the attention (you cannot say it is not striking) of a younger public, used to work with Internet.

Third cover already included the collaboration of third parties, for the release of a "definitive" third version of this book. Well, there is a fourth edition in Spanish, similar to the book you have in your hands...

Check your book

Depending on the Software you are using for eBook creation, you can introduce minor errors in the electronic file itself that can have your book blocked at the editors' web page.

For example, MsWord or LibreOffice will work flawlessly with TIFF images. You may insert them in your DOC (or ODT) file, to produce a valid PDF for paperback printing. From that DOC or ODT, you may produce an epub version with Calibre, which will keep contents and format as much as possible.

However, TIFF file format is not a valid format in standard XML, and some online retailers (for example, Apple iTunes) will reject the document. In a best case, it will be accepted, removing the image.

So it makes sense that you pass some kind of advanced control. Good news is that there is an "official" tool for this. IDPF (the International Digital Publishing Forum) has an online tool to check epub files up to 10Mb in size.

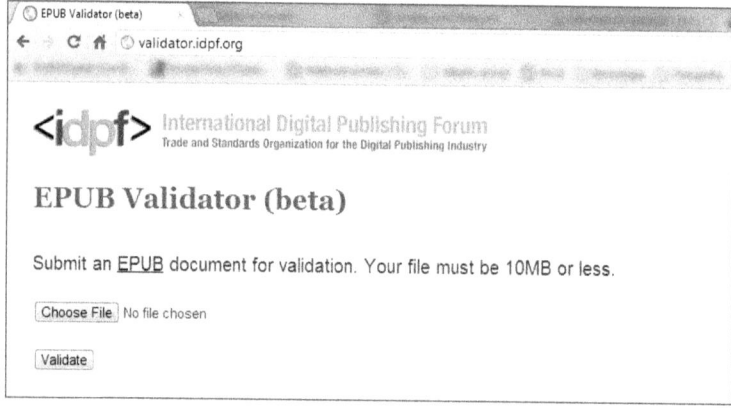

This tool (you can find it under http://validator.idpf.org) is quite simple, and all you have to do is to choose your file from your computer or drive, and click on the "Validate" button. File will be uploaded and scanned for *non-conformity* with the epub standard.

In case something is found, you will get a list of errors or issues, including the HTML chapter (remember, epubs are XML documents) and the line.

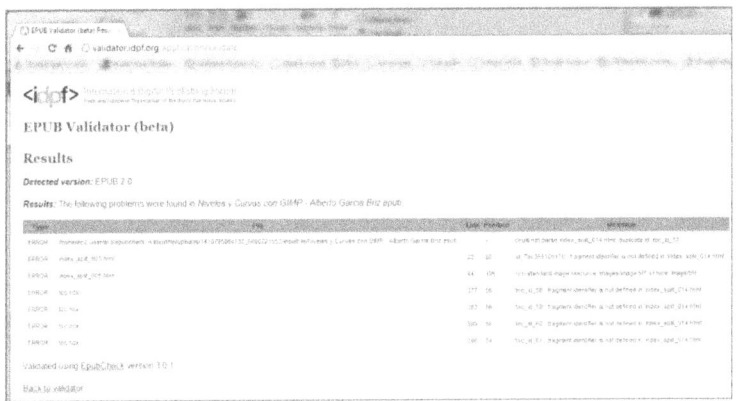

If you want to publish "many" books, you may prefer to install a local version of this tool, called EpubCheck. Current version is v3.0.1, which can be downloaded as a ZIP file (for windows) from the github web page URL https://github.com/IDPF/epubcheck/releases/tag/v3.0.1.

Source code is also available, in case you want to try and compile it for your specific operating system.

Some issues (like the above mentioned one of wrong file formats) can be easily solved, just by replacing the invalid image by a new, valid one. For some other you may need to work on the HTML code, and this may be quite tricky... For this, I use Sigil, as presented in the initial sections.

Publishing your book

Publishing process in itself is quite similar for all different online editors, either traditional, offset ones or POD printers.

The minimum personal information that they will request from you is a legal contact (name, address) and a bank account (maybe PayPal as an alternative) to process your royalty payments. In case the editor is paying via checks, this later may not even be needed...

You may want to publish using a pen name. In this case, you should look for an original name, not related to any (real) character. Do not publish as Barack Obama. Anyway, most likely you would not be allowed to...

In case you are working with some collaboration at any phase (texts edition, images, pictures, edition, layout...) you may also want to include the names in the book register.

Finally, you may need to provide some further data, at least in your first register (as in most Internet web pages).

Author or pen name?

A typical doubt in some cases is if you should use your real name or a pen name in your book. Of course, this is a personal decision. The editor will always have your "real" data, and royalties will be paid to a real person (or company). Only seldom you will find an online editor that will pay to a PayPal account without further details...

Anyway, pen names are a valid, accepted solution. Maybe you produced too much content (novels, short stories, essays) in the past and now you want to publish all that, without saturating your market.

Or maybe you work in two different areas (horror novels and cooking recipes...?) and you want to keep those independent somehow...

All is possible. The only thing you have to do is to find the right name (remember to avoid all celebrities) and use it throughout the whole process with the editor.

Usually, the register process for the author and for each new book will be independent, and you can also include several authors per book; some or all of these could be pen names, which can be good for you if you just want to use a pen name.

Anyway, before starting to look for a nice name and publishing under several pen names, read a bit more on this book, and specifically the promotion and marketing section. You might need to run several author pages on the internet, and this can be a demanding job...

Book editors...

Every day you will find new companies devoted to online edition and PDO services. Those huge, automated printers / presses allow you to enter the publishing world with just a few mouse clicks.

Concurrence is lowering costs, which is good for you and the editorial market in general. Books can be sold at "contained" prices. Still big companies have some control on this market, but the differences should reduce as the emerging market matures to a stable position.

In all cases, you may find that it is more favourable to work with companies outside your country... Let's see a first list of POD companies (at the end of this book you have a list of Internet links):

- **Amazon.com**, based in US, it runs parallel divisions in several countries: Germany, Brazil, Canada, Spain, France, India, Italy, Japan... they are one of the reference parts in electronic books, mainly oriented to their proprietary eBook reader Kindle. If you want to publish with them, you will need to look for their "Kindle Direct Publishing (KDP)" web page.
- **Autoprint.com,** based in Spain (the original edition of this book is in Spanish), it offers multiple publishing options, apart from books: cards, stationery, posters... Prices are relatively high, but it can be an interesting site if you need added promotional material for your book.
- **Blurb.com** is specialised in photograph books printing, including large format and full-page (even double-page) photo printing. As specialty editor, prices are higher, but the results are also above average quality...

- **Bubok.com** has also presence in many countries, and they distribute both eBooks and paperbacks in their web, and also in third party ones.
  They have a limited number of formats, but added options such as hard cover with sleeve. Prices are relatively high.

- **CafePress.com** is another option from USA. They offer different binding options, but fewer book sizes. It can be a bit expensive at some options.

- **Casadellibro.com** works mainly in Spanish, and their objective is to be the reference in eBook publication in that language. They have their own shop, not connected to others like Amazon.

- **CreateSpace.com** is the paperback division of Amazon. Also located in the US, they have some printing facilities in Europe, both continental and UK. Many different book sizes and good royalties…

- **Draft2Digital** is another American company, but their business model is centred on distribution. Through them, you can centralize your sales in Amazon and iTunes, for example. They work with eBooks only.

- **Finisterraediciones.com** is a Spanish company with good potential, but with some major issues. They will not sell your book worldwide, for example. However, they also have traditional presses, so that the shift to mass printing can be really easy…

- **GooglePlay,** from Google. Quite a hidden option, you can of course register as author in GooglePlay and upload your books as epub or PDF (they only work in electronic format) to sell them in their online shop.

- **iTunes / iBooks**, from Apple. Same concept as for the music, you can sell your books there, too. They have their own tools (iTunes Producer and iBooks author) to create (or convert to) their proprietary format, so that books can be read on iPads, iPhones and so. An interesting market…

- **IngramSpark,** this is a good option if you want to print small batches (from 50 units they will not charge the processing costs, a $49 value for paperback and eBook). Competitive pricing and many binding and cover options.

- **Lulu.com,** also an American company with worldwide reach. They offer a wide variety of format and binding, but prices are slightly high, so they can make periodic sale campaigns.
- **Neobooks,** German company with distribution all over Europe, but mainly in German-speaking countries. They can also sell through Amazon and iTunes (acting as integrators), so this could spare you some work. Their website is in German only.
- **NookPress,** from Barnes & Noble (one of the biggest American book retailer), they sell eBooks for their own reader device, the nook. They have also a European site, based in the UK.
- **Pubit.com,** also dependent on Barnes & Noble, it is currently in the process of merging with NookPress.
- **SmashWords,** also an integrator with their own online store. A good channel to sell on iTunes, for example. Their commission is similar to that of other integrators.
- **WattPad.com,** based in Canada. They sell eBooks only, and their members database (both readers and writers) is already over one million people – a good potential for marketing and networking.

Many of these editors may have a local facility or office in your country. And, most likely, you will be able to set the web language to your own one. If you are lucky, printing will also be made locally, so that delivery costs and times will be reduced.

Of course, you might also find some local editor which is not listed here – as commented, everyday there are more and more online editors / printers. In spite of higher costs, you may prefer to work with somebody who is "just around the corner", speaking your own language...

Traditional editors
An important fact, that was already visible in the 2013 Frankfurt Book Fair, is that traditional book editors are moving fast into the electronic book market and self-publication.

Most of them have already their proposals and products in their web pages. Still some adaptation to the "all open" trend in Internet is missing, so you may still need to provide your full data before receiving information on their terms and conditions.

To the editors listed in the previous section, we can add the following ones, as more traditional editors:

- **Authonomy,** from Harper Collins. Inside the *Authoright* platform, they will ask just too many questions before even showing you their pricing.
- **Author Solutions,** already named in the section above, dependent on Penguin.
- **Epubli.de,** a German company dependent on Holtzbrink, they do both paperback and eBook distribution. Prices are well described (ISBN costs 14.95€…) and are quite fair, with many options for the paper versions.
- **NeoBooks,** also from Holtzbrink, named in the previous section.
- **RocaAutores,** from the Spanish editor Roca Editorial. As most newcomers, their prices are really high… They *force you* to hire their different services (proofreading, edition) before publishing your book "for free".
- **Writers & Artists,** from Bloomsbury. Added to their own services, they provide a search tool for local editors and printers. This can be very useful depending on where you live, or if you have some special book in mind.

Private Editors

With the current economic crisis, you will also find people in Internet that will offer their services for proofreading and edition (even me, the author, can be contacted for that!) at reasonable fares.

In this case, you may find people that will offer you the moon, with incredible quality levels in the shortest lead times. Everything to get your attention.

Or you may find quite picky people that will first screen your work to decide if it is eligible to be processed by them. And this can even be the excuse to charge you extra money!

If you decide to go for a personal editor, make sure you have some references, or maybe you can check a sample of his / her work. In many cases, it will be much better that you review your work again, or maybe some friends or family members. Believe me, they will still find errors you did not see in your first fifty revisions.

Free publication

Contents publishing at zero cost (and zero income!) may need a separate comment, here. You may want to publish something just for the sake of it, and you do not intend to make money out of your hobby (in my opinion, this would not be completely right).

Or rather, you may want to publish certain amount of data or documents free of charge, so that your target readers get to know you.

In these cases, you will find many online shops and webs that can offer your book(s) free of charge to the readers. This way, your creation will be available to the general public, without the need to end in piracy or illegal downloading.

Process will be very similar to that of commercial editors (in fact, most of those will also offer your free books, if you ask them to). You will need to provide some basic personal data, a nickname (if you want to use one) and the electronic file in the required format.

Here you can see a list of web pages, many of them offering publications in multiple languages (this being a new possibility for your books, as indicated in previous sections):

- **24symbols:** Platform that offers online books reading (no download service, here).
- **BiblioEteca:** Based on user recommendations, it works as a social network.
- **Biblioteca Digital Hispánica:** Initiative of the Spanish National Library, it offers access to thousands of scanned historic documents.
- **CSIC (Spain):** The Consejo Superior de Investigaciones Científicas (High Counsel for Scientific Research) has a dedicated section for free books to read in its libraries network. Most books are related to technical topics.

- **Europeana:** A huge European library with lots of books and videos available online.

- **Librear:** Web with free books with different access rights: Creative Commons, Copyleft or public domain.

- **Librodot:** With a database limited to "just" over 11,000 books, they ofer mostly fiction books.

- **Libroteca:** Their catalogue contains multiple areas and topics, including some modern books and works from Nobel prizes.

- **OpenLibrary:** Worldwide initiative to promote reading, it includes both free and paid books.

- **Gutemberg Project:** They store more than 40,000 references, including ancient documents, maps, daily press...

- **The Internet Archive:** Similar to the Gutemberg Project web.

- **Wikisource:** A concept similar to OpenLibrary, it includes a big amount of free books, some of them in PDF format.

If you make an Internet search, you will find new sites almost every day, similar to the above ones.

An important point here, though. Many commercial editors include a clause in their contracts indicating that you must inform them on any price reduction on any external web site. This way, if you sell an eBook in Amazon at 2.99€ and you offer it for free somewhere else, you need to advice Amazon on this change.

In the specific case of Amazon, this would mean that the work is considered public domain, and then you cannot claim your author royalties for the "free" sales, once the price has been updated. You must read the small writing on the contract of your usual sales channel.

Decisions...

When it comes to selecting a specific editor for your paperback book (and as I say, check again the Internet, you may find somebody new), you will need to consider different fundamental topics. For example, you may want to review the following:

- **Manufacturing costs**, which will be usually the price you can buy your own books at (removing all editor benefit and your royalty). This is important if you will buy your own production for later distribution, be it on the Internet or in a local shop. In case of eBooks, this could be related to file size, which implies electronic storage and delivery costs.

- **Your margin as author**, typically a percentage of the final selling price, or rather the "remaining part" after taking out manufacturing, delivery costs and editor commission.

- **Available distribution channels** where you want to market your book. Frequently, editors will have a direct channel to main online shops as Amazon or iTunes, but they may charge you some commission (either a fix quantity or a percentage on the book price) for data handling. Access to physical libraries and bookstores is usually charged, too, since the seller's commission is also added.

- **Available book formats,** in case you have some special idea in mind (mostly for paper editions), out of standard print sizes, or maybe paper quality, binding...

- **Book contents.** It will be a very different process the production of a pocket paperback novel or a big-sized photo book. Some editors are specialized in a certain type of books.

- **Editor's support.** Nowadays, most online editors include some manuals and how-to documents that will help you creating your final product. Some editors also include a forum where you may contact other authors.

- **Professional services.** If you don't see yourself capable of doing some of the publishing steps (for example, cover creation), many editors will provide you with contacts to designers and publishing professionals, at reasonable rates.

In the end, decision is only yours. Depending on the type of book you are preparing, your target reader, the desired output quality... you may prefer working with one specific editor or the other, and this might change from a book to the next one.

Recommendation here could be to try different publishing platforms, if you do not come to a clear decision. However, we will see later on that royalties' generation is a long run, and you may prefer to stick to a single editor...

If you just want to publish a single book, many of the above listed topics may not apply to you – then, decision is much easier...

Taxes from USA

Many of the companies listed previously (Lulu, Amazon, Create-Space...) are based in the United States of America. In principle, since you are exploiting the global possibilities offered by Internet, this should not be a problem.

The company will be able to send you a check to cover your royalties, or maybe they will do a bank transfer or even a PayPal payment.

However, there is a small fiscal issue here. US Government (as most other countries) requests that companies declare all payment done as wages, royalties, author copyright... inside their country. So your benefit (no matter where you really live) will be registered in the US tax system.

Problem here is that default withholding is the highest rate possible – in this case, a 30%. Then, if you do not do a couple of things, you will just get a 70% of your share...

Of course, there are ways to avoid this. Many international, bilateral treaties try to avoid double taxing (of course, you should declare income in your country of residence). Most likely, your country will have one of these treaties in place.

But you have to demonstrate that you live in that country, and that you are yourself (?). You must request to be applied a specific treaty...

> *Note: In the meantime, companies such as Amazon and CreateSpace allow for the introduction of a foreign tax identification number, so that you may spare all paperwork I will describe below.*

Step by step

Starting point is to register as physical person in the US tax system. To do so, you must fill-in a **W-7 form** (you may download all this information from www.irs.gov), together with a certified copy of your passport.

> *Important: you must fill-in the form fully. If you live outside the US, you must indicate two different options:*
>
> *- Checkbox A, to indicate that you are a foreigner, not living in the US, and that you claim to be applied a tax treaty.*
>
> *- Checkbox H, indicating "Exception 1d: Third party withholding on passive income (royalties)"*

It is also recommended to add a letter from your editor (don't worry, you can usually download and print them from your editor's web page), in order to justify that you will be working "for them", and they will pay you the royalties, subject to taxes.

By doing so, you will get your ITIN – *Income Taxpayer Identification Number*. But this does not end here...

Once you have your ITIN, you may feed it into the W8-BEN form (available at the same web page), which is the means to request the exemption to double taxation. This means, in a first step, that you will not be applied the initial 30% tax withholding.

Real tax will then be paid in your country, and amount to pay will be most likely much lower.

For example, withholding tax for publications is 5% (8% in case of scientific publications). In Germany, it is 0%. All paperwork is worth is, isn't it?

An important data, from the way IRS works you need to send a dedicated W8-BEN form to each different editor. CreateSpace is a company inside the Amazon group, but if you want to publish both paperback and eBook versions you will need to send two forms – one to each entity.

> *Note: Even when sometimes you cannot avoid it, many people is reluctant to provide some private data.*
>
> *You do not need to provide an ITIN number, nor sending a W8-BEN form – if you don't mind losing that 30% tax withholding...*

IRS provides all documents (and instructions on how to fill them in) both in English and Spanish.

Selling an eBook

All right, so you have your book (interior and cover) ready. You even made an epub check, and everything seems to be OK. Now it is the time to send the files to your editor.

Just in case, you should check the size of your files. Remember that images will add much "weight" to the documents, and preferably they should be adapted to the target reader device – typically, around 600 pixels wide for pocket readers.

And there are two reasons to insist in this file size topic. First, we already saw that increasing image dimensions will not improve rendering on the screen. It can even make the reading experience *sluggish,* with longer page-loading times.

But second reason is that many online editors will charge a certain amount based on the file size, which has to be stored and transferred to the buyer. For example, Amazon takes around 0.12€ per Megabyte. We will see how this affects you in a few moments.

Book register

But first thing you have to do is to register the book on the editor's system. You will need to provide the title and author's name, and select the preferred option for ISBN assignment (none, own, editor's). In case of ebooks, you may not need an ISBN in your country.

> **Note**: Remember that the ISBN of an electronic publication must be different from the one in the paper version.

After that, you will need to upload the files, either as produced or re-formatted by some online converter. The editor will check the files, and it can take a couple of days until you receive a confirmation on the validity of the book to be distributed.

At that point, you should be able to review the "final" document, either by downloading a copy of the epub (or mobi) file or by proofing in an online viewer. Remember that your book may be sold for different devices, so it might not render properly in some of those.

If you confirm that the book is right, you will be moved on to the price configuration.

Setting a price

And here is where the file size does matter. To set the price for your eBook, you will need to consider, at least, the three following numbers:

- **File cost,** for example as indicated in previous sections (0.12€/Mb at Amazon). This should cover their costs for storage, data management and delivery to the buyer.
- **Editor's commission,** usually a variable amount with some defined minimum.
- **Your own share as author royalty.**

These three figures define the final selling price (plus the specific country taxes, where it applies). Typically, editor's share is low (they make business selling lots of books), so prices can also be low – depending on the royalties you expect.

> **Example**: Amazon provides a 70% royalty (from sales price) for sales in Europe. A book that is 1.8Mb will have fixed costs (2014) of 0.12 x 1.8 = 0.22€. Due to this "high" cost, Amazon indicates a minimum selling price of 2.99€ in Europe.
>
> If you decide to take that minimum price, you will get 2.09€ per book sold. Amazon will get 2.99 – 2.09 – 0.22 = 0.68€
>
> If you sell that a book at 3.99€, your royalty increases to 2.79€, and Amazon's share would raise to 3.99 – 2.79 – 0.22 = 0.98€

Of course, you can set the price as high as you want. In all cases, current trend is to sell eBooks at a lower price than paperback versions – mainly a psychological thing: you would remove materials and printing costs.

Following the previous calculations, if you really have a killer book nothing prevents you to sell it (say) at 9.99€, then your royalties would be 6.99€ **per book**. Not bad, huh? But you have to consider that you must compete with millions of books... so visibility will be a big point. We will come to that in later sections.

Lending, promotion

Even when you set a minimum price, usually considering the royalty per sold eBook, you have to think of some alternatives for promotion (mainly, in the biggest platforms) where you would want to reduce your benefits in order to gain more visibility.

This way, Amazon does have a lending program for its Prime members. In that case, the user does not pay anything for the book (which is returned a few days later). Instead, Amazon pays the authors a certain amount for each lending.

You can also prepare promotions, specific time slots when your book will be sold with a discount (reduction comes from your share...), or rather fully free. Again, it is visibility we are after.

DRM (Digital Rights Management)

A decision you will have to make is if you want to copy-protect your books. Some editors such as Amazon and Apple provide s way to control the distribution of your electronic books.

At the sale process, data on the purchase itself is added to the eBook, usually including information on the buyer and the list of registered or authorized reader devices to store and show your book.

Use of DRM is not compulsory, but many people consider it to be the way to fight piracy.

On the other side, you have to reckon that DRM protection can be eventually cracked. And adding DRM protection to your books may stop certain readers from purchasing it. Some buyers may be reluctant to provide personal data, or information on their owned devices.

In the end, this will be your own personal decision. You must consider pros and cons... and anyway, DRM can be removed in a re-publish process.

Multiple publication

In the previous section I already included a list of different eBook and paperback editors. Each one has a special way of working, and they will impose certain initial conditions.

However, some of the strictest conditions (such as exclusivity) can be avoided.

A possible strategy is to create different file formats (which will be considered as different documents), so that you may upload a ".mobi" to Amazon, then an ".epub" to iTunes and Google Play, and finally you may sell your PDF file in your personal web page.

As you will understand, the required effort increases as you add more and more distributors to your work. Some of them may request that you use one of their ISBN numbers, which could make some specific format not valid for other editors.

Specifically, the personal web page (I will go back to this later on) can be an issue at the beginning, since you will need a secure payment connection and you will have to comply with current data protection laws. If you like to program web pages, this can be an interesting exercise; else, you may hire this service on any Internet hosting provider.

Decision on specific editors or resellers will again be a personal one; it can also depend on the type of book, your target public and country... Anyway, the generic advice is to try to achieve as much coverage as possible, to reach the maximum number of potential readers (and purchasers).

Selling a paperback

Print on demand adds some problems to these of electronic book publication.

Specialization of some editors (for example, CreateSpace does not do pocket books, Blurb is specialized in high-end finishing for photography or art books), the need of a logistics channel and the reach to physical stores can influence the whole process.

And you must take into account that you need to provide input in many "new" areas in a paperback edition. Composition and layout will be as you designed, with specific font faces, colours and contents distribution.

This way, draft proofreading is even more important than for eBooks, before your official release for printing. Again, you are responsible for the creation of high quality contents (image resolution, colours used, if any...) and layout must respect all requirements from the specific editor. If not, you may find that your book is rejected and you have to modify it to comply with these requirements anyway.

Usually, editors will offer the possibility of printing a single first book for you to check (you will pay only manufacturing costs and delivery), so you can make sure that the printing and binding processes respect your original concept.

Upon reception of the proof simple, you must check the contents and layout, but also binding and book finish...

Process is similar to that for eBooks: you upload your files to the editor web page (interior and cover), you define minimum price and royalty and submit it for technical revision.

A couple of days after, you will receive a notice for you to review the received data (the editor may introduce minor modifications) in order to approve the sample and agreed prices.

Proofreading interchange

An interesting activity could be proofreading interchange. Some editors include different forums where you can meet authors like you, willing to review your unpublished work if you do the same for them. So they can find these errors you did not upon your thousandth revision.

Of course, this activity implies certain level of confidence in the other authors. You are distributing your work before publishing it, and you have to make sure your counterpart is a serious person. You may decide to split your work and have it reviewed partially by several people in parallel.

Anyway, it is another way to gain visibility among people like you, getting to know "first hand" if your book is good even before releasing it for printing... And they may also help you in promoting your work.

A different way to proofread...

If you speak different languages, a nice way to review your work is to translate it into a new language. The level of abstraction achieved upon converting the phrases and language structures can help you find missed typographic errors, wrong sentences...

Differences

Obviously, publishing in paper is not the same thing as doing an eBook. On one side, the effort behind is much bigger, especially if you prepared a complex layout.

You may need to spend some more time in the edition and preparation of your (high-resolution) images, to reach the requested quality.

Still, this is not just a matter of file sizes and resolutions. A very important decision will be the selection of the physical sales channels for the distribution of your work.

Bookstores and libraries will typically add some commission to the book price, which means added costs for the availability in normal street stores.

At least, your book will be added to some global database, so any book store will be able to find it and request it to the editor, if they do not have it on their shelves. This added step in the logistics chain is what you pay with the bookstore commission.

Then, the difference between selling just online or in bookstores can be as high as a 30% of the final price. If you do not want to increase prices that much, you will have to consider reducing your royalties accordingly.

> **Note**: *sales margin allows bookstores and online shops applying later discounts on specific dates or products, sales seasons...*

Again, it is your decision. Depending on the type of book, you may be interested in being listed in the databases of the main bookstores (such as Barnes & Noble and Hugendubel), or in the ones of the main distributors, such as Baker and Taylor or Ingram.

You will have to decide whether to get fewer royalties per book but a wider visibility, with increased sales possibilities... considering that no sale is assured. Again, it is all image and visibility.

In general, and depending on the number of distribution channels that you pick in a given editor, you will find that the obtained royalty will be different if the book was sold directly by the editor (commission "A"), through web sites like Amazon (commission "A" plus "B") or rather at a physical bookstore (commissions "A", "B" and "C").

Setting the price for a paperback

Starting point will be similar to that of an eBook. In the previous section, I spoke about file cost, editor commission and margin for the author.

Well, now we have a reference cost defined by the manufacturing costs (printing and binding) of your book.

If we spoke before about cost per megabyte of information, now the number of pages, the book size and the type of binding selected will typically define cost. In every editor webpage, you may find a calculator to estimate manufacturing costs and commercial margin.

But, as I just commented, we have to add not the share for every step in the distribution of the physical sample. The margin added by the bookstore will reduce your potential royalty at a given selling price, if you do not want to increase it.

If you are going to sell your books yourself (at least, a first launch promotion), you will also have to add packaging and postage costs, and (in some cases) different taxes (see note in the following pages).

Is bookstore distribution really worth it?

In many cases, you will find that your editor (for example, CreateSpace in the USA) provides a direct channel to local bookstores… in the USA.

Of course, stores in your country can find your book (if you select that option) through an ISBN search. If a customer asks for your book, the shop will be able to order it, so that it can be received in the physical store a few days later.

> *Note*: *Most commercial distribution channels (for CreateSpace, this is called "Extended Distribution Channel", EDC) can only work with a reduced set of book sizes and types.*
>
> *Check this with your editor before starting some complex book layout…*

However, POD editors give lower margins to bookstores, compared with traditional printers. And, in most cases, they have a non-return police in place, so bookstores are not eager to buy batches of POD books, unless you are a successful writer. They will not risk the initial investment needed.

So the decision to select a specific distribution channel to reach a potential wider audience is on you, again. It will depend on your country, target public, type of book… There is no universal "rule of thumb" for this.

Personal promotion

But remember that you will be able to buy your own books at production costs' price.

Once you have a firs box of books at home, nothing prevents you from selling them yourself, be it on Internet, in a local market or library, or at your friend's bar. Or even in a real bookstore, so that you will show that buying a (small) batch is worth it.

To get your public to know you, you may sell these books at a lower price than the recommended sales price for commercial channels – still with some benefit for you.

Anyway, this kind of retail sale is not the best option at mid-term, because of the effort needed (time, third-party space usage, small benefit from a small batch…)

In the next section we will see what we can do to improve our sales from home.

Online shops and subcontracting

Of course, you can prepare your own online shop inside your author web page (both being recommended actions, both the web and the shop). This way you can extend the personalized sale for a while.

You can have a small stock of books at home, bought at author's cost, and then sell them with the above discussed pricing considerations. However, you have some other options available.

In case you want to set a personal shop inside the Amazon framework, they will make sure your books appear in the search tool, and they will inform you on every sale your channel achieves. But, how about if they took care of everything?

Amazon logistics

An interesting option inside the online giant is that you can fully use their logistics chain. And, most important, you do not need to edit or print your book with them: it is an independent, paid service that you may link anyway, if you want to.

This service, named "Fulfilment by Amazon", allows you to send your stock to their warehouse(s), who will then process the orders and shipments in the very same way as for Amazon purchases.

You just have to keep that stock available in their warehouse, paying for the delivery costs – an added cost for your calculations. Furthermore, Amazon will charge you a "shelf space rental" to maintain the logistic process and tool in place.

Financing

As I already commented in previous sections, initial costs for paperback publishing are really low, even zero in some cases. However, sometimes it is recommended to make some investment upon starting a new project.

Depending on the type of book, initial unit costs can be high: graphic novels, photo books in colour... will imply high prices from the very first copy.

Possible discount in "high" quantities (say, from 100 units on) can be good, but this means you will need to make an important first payment if, for example, you intend to sell from your own web site.

This way, it is common to use some external source for financing. Your specific project may suggest going to some big company or association, in search of the required budget, or at least a part of it.

Example cases would be if you are presenting or using products of the company in your publication, or if you are publishing a photo book with images of a given city or specific place (then you can ask in the local town hall).

Crowdfunding

But, since you are working already with Internet, you may also want to go to some social funding network, the so-called crowdfunding.

This social funding can be found typically in specific web sites where you need to register to present your project, with a detail of the idea, expected costs and timeframe to realize it.

Besides, you may already suggest the amounts each investor or donor should provide, maybe with some reward related to the level of investment.

> *Note*: this point is important. You must decide the role of your helpers in your promotion.

> *An investor can expect to get some benefit out of his / her inversion. For example, to receive a sample of your work upon publishing, for free or at a reduced price.*
>
> *A donor may not expect anything from his investment, maybe just read his / her name in the book credits. Amounts are typically smaller, but you should not dismiss them.*

And here is where a wholesale discount can be interesting for you. If you offer your book at a reduced price during your campaign, you will attract investors easier. But this forces you to buy this minimum amount in advance, which will define you initial expenses.

As in some other cases, you may offer different products in a given campaign, or rather a same product with different finishing, for example:

- Paperback version of your book
- Hardcover version of your book, maybe in a bigger format
- Hardcover version, big format and some additional material, such as a poster or selected pictures to frame.

Of course, you can use this strategy for whatever publication you have in mind. It does not need to be a full-colour graphic book.

You can also use crowdfunding for an electronic book, if you plan to have some initial expenses (such as a subcontracted cover design, or a translation to the target language) you cannot afford.

Anyway, the process is exactly the same as the one already indicated. In some cases, you will be requested to provide more information (personal data, PayPal account...), or even the country of residence, for the legal conditions may change from country to country.

Crowdfunding companies

Below you can find a list of some web sites that offer crowdfunding services. You may visit them, to see how other authors do present their projects – and not only books, but also music records, art work, travels... you will find the links to these web sites at the end of this book.

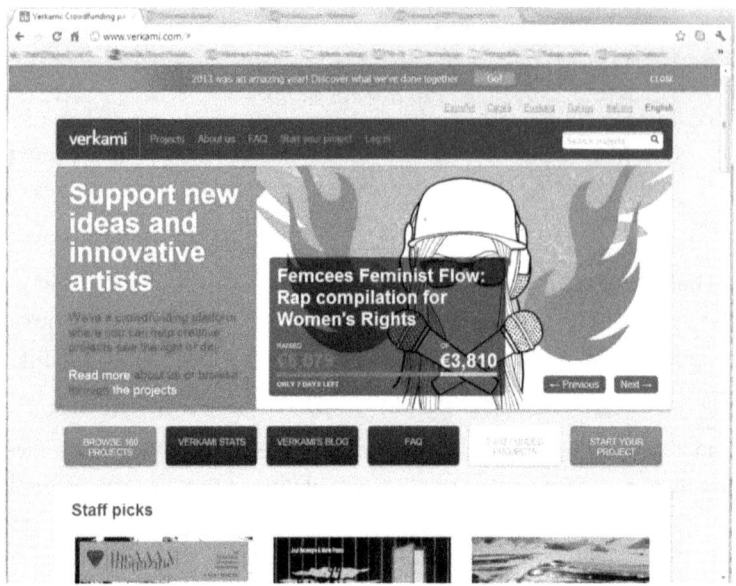

Verkami.com is the Spanish reference in terms of social funding platforms

All of them will charge you some commission (around 3% to 5%) on your budget, which you have to take into account in your total cost estimations. Some of them will charge you even if you do not achieve your goal.

I recommend you to visit several platforms before deciding a specific one.

- **Crowdfunder,** British platform for all types of artworks.
- **Crowdtilit,** based in the USA, they give you the option to decide what to do with the money if you do not reach your goal.
- **FundAnything,** also American, they accept all kinds of projects, including personal or charity ones.
- **IndieGoGo,** started as an indie-film crowdfunding site, now they accept other types of artwork, including publications.
- **Kickstarter,** maybe the most known site, working since 2009. Lately with bad reviews due to their blocking of some "big" achieved projects' funding. 99% of the proposals work just fine, though. Mainly operation in the USA.
- **Lanzanos,** Spanish initiative for artistic creations without a lucrative goal.

- **Pozible,** they allow you to propose your project funding in BitCoins, or one-to-one funding projects. They have offices in the USA, Australia, Malaysia and Singapore.
- **StartNext,** German web site, mainly working on projects from that country. Interesting if you are targeting that market.
- **Verkami,** successful Spanish platform for all kinds of creative projects.

An important point here. The above list includes just a few of the current crowdfunding platforms. Every day you can find more and more new platforms, some of them oriented to specific markets or projects.

The above list does not include, for example, platforms dedicated to industrial or company investment. This might be an alternative for you, if you intend to edit and publish third-party books or contents.

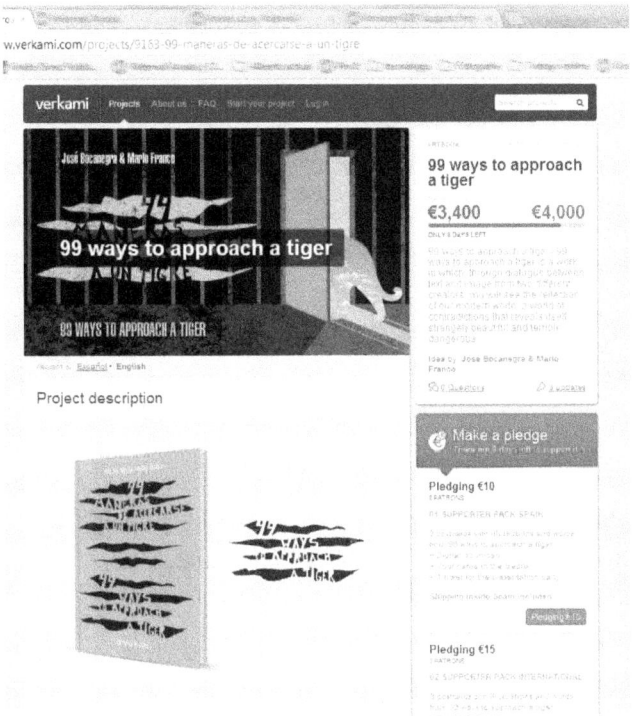

Example of Project proposal in Verkami (in Spanish). Look at the list of different amounts on the lower-right side.

Seat down and wait? No!

So your editor has checked the file and has accepted it. You set a price, and confirm (personally and electronically) that the book is right, maybe after a few revisions. What now?

Usually, your book will appear in a few hours or days in the distribution channels you selected in the registration process (publisher's web page, external webs, physical book shops...) after submission of the files.

Being it Print-on-demand, usually book stores will request (if any!) just a few copies of your book. Usually, they will only place an order if a reader asks for your book.

Anyway, your editor will track all your sales for each different channel. You will be able to access this information (with more or less detail) as often as you want, with an indication on your royalties' share earned so far.

Most editors set minimum thresholds for the payment (for example, 10€ for wire transfer, then 100€ for paper checks), so some time may pass before you "see" any money from your sales.

Some editors (such as Amazon) added some minor issue in the past, since all different sites worked independently and threshold had to be reached separately to get royalties from a specific site. Royalties were not cumulative.

> *Note: In the meantime, Amazon has removed the thresholds for electronic money transfers.*

Even when you reach the specified threshold, payment can still be delayed if the editor has to withhold your taxes, prepare your official (electronic) invoice and do the transfer itself.

So your best option is to try and sell your book well, and as soon as possible, knowing that results will only be visible some weeks or months later. You need to move on.

Marketing, promotion, networking

Your editor will most likely post a link to your book in its own web site. It will be listed in their search tool, and they may even register it in bigger online shops such as Amazon.

Still, it can be difficult for your potential readers to find among the millions of books available in online stores. Maybe the kind of book is not usual for the selected editor (in my case, CreateSpace does a lot of novels, but few practical or technical books like this one).

Anyway, you should take responsibility on the promotion of your own work if you are not a famous writer. This will mean defining a "global" Internet-presence strategy, so that the information on your new book can reach the maximum number of potential customers.

Here you can find a list of recommendations towards the definition of your own strategy (in fact, similar to those needed for any other online business):

- Create (or contract) **your own author's webpage**, to provide some reference on your works, maybe a more general view on your profile and links to other sites of (your) interest. This way, you will be closer to your potential readers.

- Create a **Facebook Page** (important: not a personal profile). Here you can get followers that can be informed periodically on your progress, presentations, new publications… besides, this is a safe communications channel (you do not need to provide personal email addresses, for example).

- If you use it, create a **dedicated Twitter account** to add one more channel to your readers. This can also be used to announce public events with very short notice.

- Contract (if you have the budget) an **online advertisement campaign**, such as Google AdWords. References to your book will appear in related searches according to parameters you can define (gender, age, personal interest of the person making the search…).

- Create **your own blog**, to keep your presence online (in a similar way as your Facebook page). Write on related topics, even if it is not on your own production: book fairs, meetings, events related to the topics in your books...

- Participate in **editor's forums,** in order to contact authors with similar profiles than yours, to share experiences and to give or get help in editing or publishing topics.
- **Collaborate with other writers**, proofreading their work and letting them do so with yours. As previously indicated, this is a nice way to meet people with similar interests to yours.
- **Investigate further options,** such as Goodreads.com, a portal (bought by Amazon) where readers and writers recommend books and interchange opinions on the books they have read.
- ...

Networking

Active participation in editor's forums (or other specialised ones) will allow you to be known to specific, reduced groups with higher potential to "connect" with your ideas.

> **Note**: Editor's forums usually have a thread or section to present new publications. It is not polite to spam all groups with commercial information on your new book...

A good way to increase your online presence can be the link interchange with other authors of similar books, creating a network of contacts that will allow you to reach a wider public – and usually oriented to your topics, already.

Of course, you can decide to go for professional networks such as LinkedIn or Xing, if you want to focus your career on writing or editing.

An intermediate step, already hinted, would be to contact other authors directly; together with cross-proofing, you may interchange blog posts or links to personal webpages, to increase traffic.

On one side, this may lead your followers to external sites, but on the other side you will get new traffic to your place. You have to balance pros and cons...

Promotion

Editors will typically allow you to change the pricing of your books from time to time, both for paperback and electronic versions. Of course, at a reduction of your royalty.

Even when you should not change prices frequently (and at your cost!), you may use this as a commercial strategy when planning a new release, or on specific dates.

Anyway, a good campaign on your online sites (personal web, Facebook, blog...) can bring some interesting sales at a given time point.

And this applied also to old versions of a book. You might want to keep it on sale, at a lower price. You will get lower royalties, but the number of different publications will remain higher than if you remove the old book completely.

Once again, it is your decision, but you should consider visibility as a main driver for your online sales.

Intellectual Property register

Many authors do not pay much attention to this point at the beginning. In old, traditional press times, you had to take a couple of copies of your printed book to some special place (for example, to a state library) to certify your authorship and protect the contents.

Currently, the register process of electronics books can be much simpler (depending on your country). You might already have some way to make it online (including books addition to databases), through some private companies such as SafeCreative.

If you had some legal problem in the future (for example, somebody copies your work or a part of it without your permit) this registry will help you to demonstrate authorship.

Of course, protection coverage can have different levels or categories, but even free accounts can be used to define your book's publication date, a critical item in legal discussion.

Traditional paperback register is also recommended. You will need to find the right organisation in your country. For example, in Spain you can file in your request through the Ministry for Education and Culture (www.mcu.es), by filling-in a form, paying some minor taxes and providing one sample of your work. In Germany, process is similar but you have to provide two samples.

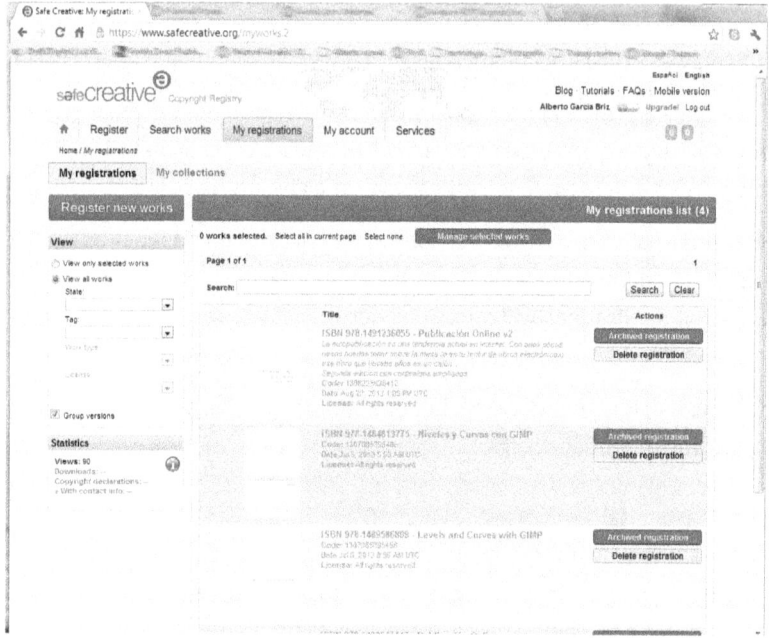

Registering your book in an appropriate platform is very easy and highly recommendable...

And this is one of the advantages of printing on demand: to do this filing, you can have just a few units printed, in order to provide them to the legal entity even before approving it for online sales.

Personal experience

In my case, for many years I had a secret project in my mind: to teach digital edition and photography, and to keep learning from that. I am passionate about both and I think I am calm enough to be able to explain topics in an interesting, fun way.

For several years, I started draft after draft, correcting them, editing, preparing images and graphics... and keeping all that in heaps of CDs and

USB sticks. But one day I found a clean working line that could integrate most of that: Photographic edition for black and white conversion.

Film development was one of my youth hobbies, using a basic laboratory that I had available at home from my dad. So I spend time over three years to create new texts, recovering old ones, creating a new layout (I changed it three times), doing hundreds of step-by-step screen captures...

Finally, I could publish my first book, "**Blanco y Negro con The GIMP**" (Black and White with The GIMP), as paperback through CreateSpace (you can see a reference to it at the end of this book).

I just sold a few (very few!) books in Amazon, but that was enough for me. I still have some sales of that book from time to time. I know it has some errors (you never get rid of those completely), but I considered it to be a final version. Still, I am working in a big update for it, and an English version is in the plan, too...

From that point, next project was a bit more technical, this time including already input from different webs and blogs. I tested multiple techniques and processes before I released "**Niveles y Curvas con GIMP**" (Levels and Curves with GIMP, also available in English). Again, photo edition. The book is smaller, indeed, maybe half the size of the first one.

But there were to positive changes, here. First, I prepared a full version in English, which can still be found in Amazon. It was my first time publishing in that language.

Second, it was also the first time I published an electronic book. Preparing the electronic version made me learn a lot on new topics (most of them included in this book), from price setting to DRM. File conversion was also a new topic for me, with the use of specific applications such as Calibre.

But once you publish your first book, you will discover you cannot stop creating new contents. In my case, I restarted my "notes on photography", still unpublished. And soon after that I started preparing the first version of this book, when I realised how many people was interested in book publication.

Every new book and version has added more and more content, updates and changes in my blogs, personal web site and Facebook page; and of course I always add the list of my latest books at the end of very new one, as a marketing strategy.

> **Note**: *This "non-invasive" marketing strategy is a good way to promote your work without putting all your family and friends against you...*

By the way, so far I did not hire any advertisement campaign with Google (AdWords) or any other company... of course, my sales are also not impressive at all. The proposals listed in previous sections are just that: proposals.

Time goes by...

Since my first publication in August 2012, I have grown personally, with my books and online publication.

Sales start to show (fall 2014) an increase in eBook compared with paperback versions. Still each type of book can have its public and a preferred support (for example, my first book would render very poorly in an eBook reader). I recommend that you analyse all available options for your publications.

And do not forget about promotion. It is a long run... just a few people will have a quick success in a short time. In reality, it can take several months until you see (relatively) good sales. Important is to keep the spirit high.

In my case, I started with a few books per month. But the addition of more sales channels, an integrator (Draft2Digital) and new books started to make income a reality.

Conclusions

Self-publishing is becoming a clear trend (together with 3D printing), mostly for new, indie writers. Maybe it is not the optimal way to publish if you intend to make money with your books. But it is definitely a good way to produce small batches for family and friends, for some specific activity or to have some minimum sales to (partially) fund your next computer or vacation.

Of course, self-publishing has a hedonist side, for personal realization. Thousands of people like you and me do publish thousands of books every year that, with some luck, will be interested to a few people. And only a few authors a year achieve relative success outside the traditional editors, which still control the mainstream market.

But the very fact of having published something will remain, forever. And it was you.

Print on demand has the advantage that a book is only produced if somebody requests it. A print is done, or an electronic file is transmitted to the buyer. No storage, no stock, no initial investment or environmental concerns – if nobody buys it, it will not be printed.

And it is really possible to write something, give it some nice "shape" and to have it on the table a few days or weeks after. Furthermore, in POD each book is unique in itself: typically, print date is written in the book.

Even first releases of your book (a draft before correction, or an old version) can become "cult items" for your fans. Why not?

Of course, looking at the commercial side, together with writing and editing you need to spend some time on marketing and communication, to make your book visible. Presentations, promotion.

From the way online editors pay, with payment thresholds and taxes withholding, your only chance to make self-publishing a business is your own, intensive work towards a "massive" campaign.

Of course, if you can write many good books quickly and publish them with a same editor, cumulative sales will help you reach the thresholds much faster. In case you publish with several editors, or those have separate thresholds (per country or sales channel), you might never see your money.

Anyway, most of the fun happens during this trip, from the idea to the contents creation to the layout and final promotion. Will you join me?

Oh, and one more recommendation. Read! Or, at least, check the books other people publish. Notice how the structure the contents, how they write. What edition decisions they took...

Glossary

AdWords - Advertisement system from Google which allows for the marketing of a product (in our case, a book) on web pages related to specific topics, to optimize online presence.

ASIN – Amazon Standard Identification Number, used by all the items they sell.

CD – Compact Disc. Optical digital media (read / write processes done with laser light) capable of storing up to 700Mb of information, it is still widely used for music. Currently replaced by DVD and BlueRay (and also magnetic and flash units) for data storage.

CMYK – Acronym for *Cyan, Magenta, Yellow, blacK*. It is the universal colour space used in professional printing, since it allows for the use of pure black ink, improving contrast.

CSS – Cascading Style Sheets, configuration files used in HTML to define document styles, including structures, colour and font families. It can be applied to other XML formats, such as epub for electronic books.

Dpi – dots per inch. Unit used to indicate the resolution of both input devices (scanners) and output devices (printers, screens). For screens and monitors, typical values are between 72dpi and 266dpi, whereas printing processes usually work with values between 300dpi and 1,200dpi.

To differentiate pixels from effective light emitters or ink droplets, the alternative unit "ppi" (pixels per inch) was defined.

DRM – Digital Rights Management. Intellectual property protection system based on the addition of specific data to the media file, which limits its usage possibilities to a given number of devices of the legal buyer.

eBook – Electronic book. It can refer both to the reader device and to the electronic document.

EDC – Expanded Distribution Channel. Option available in CreateSpace for the distribution of their POD books to libraries and book stores.

Epub – Standard electronic book format, it can be read nowadays by most electronic book readers, except for Amazon's Kindle.

EPS – Encapsulated Post Script, file format widely used in professional press until the broad adoption of PDF as standard. It is still a reference format for the storage and delivery of professional documents.

FTP – File transfer protocol. Internet communication protocol for the direct file transfer between two computers, by means of a dedicated communication channel (or *pipe*). Transfer speeds can approach these of the available connection limit (bandwidth).

GIMP – GNU Image Manipulation Program. OpenSource application for image and photo edition.

GNU – OpenSource operating system similar to UNIX, it was first created in 1983 as an alternative to it. Code publication allowed the appearance of different development groups, evolving quickly towards systems like Gnome.

HTML – Hyper-Text Markup Language. Text with interactive links, based on the use of labels. It is the original system for the definition of web pages, where labels were processed by web browsers to produce the desired screen layout.

HTML is in its fifth revision (HTML5), and is extending as a generic XML system (such as eBook readers) to other devices as a base for their graphic interface.

iBook - Proprietary electronic book from Apple, based on the epub standard with modified CSS files.

IPS – In-plane switching. Display technology used in some modern LCD screens.

IRS – Internal Revenue Service of the United States of America. Entity in charge of taxes generated by economic activity, their tracking and management.

ISBN – International Standard Book Number. Code used in the cataloguing and classification of non-periodic publications.

In some countries (Spain, Germany...) ISBN is compulsory for any commercial publication, including eBooks. The ISBN number of a physical publication cannot be the same as the one for the electronic version.

ISSN – International Standard Serial Number. Alternative code used currently by many libraries for books' classification.

ITIN – Income Taxpayer Identification Number. Identification number used in the USA for the declaration of personal income.

JPG – Joint Photography Experts Group, association that developed the definition of the JPG file standard, which ended up with the progressive algorithm from Fraunhofer Institut.

It is the most used image file format in Internet because of its high efficiency and low file sizes achieved. Lately it is suffering the competition of the PNG format, with similar compression ratios but without information losses.

Mobi – Electronic book format developed by the company Mobipocket, which was later on acquired by Amazon.

ODT – Open DocumenT. Open file format proposed initially from Sun Microsystems, it was adopted as OpenSource format against proprietary solutions from companies such as Microsoft.

OpenSource – Applied to code, programs and plugins that are developed in an open way. Source code is usually shared or distributed, and any further use can modify it to create an evolution of the item.

PDF – Portable Document Format. An original format from the company Adobe, it has been widely adopted as standard for the document interchange between the different operating systems and platforms.

Most image editors and graphic design programs, together with modern office suites, can export to this format directly.

PNG – Portable Network Graphic. Graphic or image format that takes the best side of several older formats to produce this new one, which is compatible with most modern web browsers.

Specifically it uses the full RGB colour space (8 bits per channel, like JPG and TIFF) and allows for a lossless compression (like GIF and TIFF), achieving reduced file sizes.

POD – Print-on-demand. Modern printing process that allows for the publication of very small batches, avoiding the generation of stock.

RAM – Random Access Memory. It is the working memory for all electronic devices; its contents are lost when power is switched off or removed.

RAW – File formats that contain all available information of a camera sensor, without any pre-processing.

They contain much more information than JPG files, and their size is also much bigger. RAW files typically work with 14 or 16 bits per pixel.

There are different "sub-formats", all considered to be RAW files, such as CR2 from Canon and the standard NEF.

RGB – Red, Green and Blue. It is the common colour representation system for screens and monitors, covering most of the visual spectrum to the human eye.

Colour generation in RGB system is done through colour addition. Since some years ago, there are derivative colour spaces, such as sRGB and AdobeRGB.

Royalty – Payment received on the given permission to an editor to produce and sell our intellectual property or creation (book, photograph, music...), equivalent to a payment on author rights.

RTF – Rich-Text Format. Evolution from TXT format that allows for the information addition of character style, font family and decoration. It is a good option to create simple publications without high format requirements (novels or essays, for example).

Serif – Decoration applied to characters in certain font families (for example, Times New Roman). It should improve readability in printed texts with small font sizes.

Suite – Set of different Software applications that are usually bundled together, so that they can interchange data easily in a direct way. For example, you will find references to the Office suites from Microsoft or LibreOffice / OpenOffice.

Adobe uses also the name suite for their bundle "Creative Suite", which includes all their programs on graphic design and image edition.

SVG – Scalable Vector Graphic. OpenSource format used, for example, by InkScape. It allows for the upsizing of elements and designs without quality loss.

TIFF – Tagged – Image File Format. Image file format that includes information tags. It is one of the first broadly adopted image formats, and it can work with the full RGB space and produce lossless compression in its files.

TXT – One of the very first text file formats, it is the simplest way to store text information. It does not include data on font family, decoration or size.

Since the generated file size is very small (no labels added), they are ideal for raw-data input to layout software.

USB – Universal Serial Bus. Standard digital communication link that allows for the connection of up to 127 devices per port. It is the current de-facto standard for peripherals, with the release 2.0 (transmission speeds up to 480Mbps).

There are already devices following a new revision 3.0, which should replace the previous one in short term. The future standard 3.1 will bring further changes, like symmetrical connectors (to avoid false plugging) and higher levels of available power, up to 100W.

VD16 – In German, *Verzeichnis der im deutschen Sprachbereich erschienenen Drucke des 16. Jahrhunderts*. It is a list of middle-age German books, specifically printed in the 16ᵗʰ century.

W-7 – Form used to request an ITIN from the US revenue service. This is needed to request the application of a specific tax withholding agreement.

W8-BEN – Request form used to obtain the application of a specific tax withholding treaty, usually dependent on the country of residence for non-US citizens.

WYSIWYG – *What-you-see-is-what-you-get*. Term used in computing on systems that can render on screen the final result that will be obtained upon printing.

They favour a much simpler edition process, since all applied changes are shown on the screen. Most modern image editors and vector graphic tools work with this strategy.

XML – eXtended Mark-up Language. It is a generalization of the HTML (which was also not an original idea...), based on the use of text labels inside the text information of a document, to define its *behaviour* and how it will be rendered on the screen or in a print-out.

Modern file formats are based in XML, such as ODT (from OpenOffice / LibreOffice) and SLA (layout file from Scribus).

Related links

Edition and Layout Software

- Adobe – www.adobe.com
- Calibre – calibre-ebook.com
- GIMP – www.gimp.org
- InkScape – www.inkscape.org
- LibreOffice – www.libreoffice.org
- Microsoft – www.microsoft.com
- OpenOffice – www.openoffice.org
- Scribus – www.scribus.net
- Scrivener - http://www.literatureandlatte.com/scrivener.php
- Sigil - http://code.google.com/p/sigil/

Editors

- Amazon – kdp.amazon.com
- Authonomy – http://authonomy.com
- Author Solutions – www.authorsolutions.com
- Autoprint – www.autoprint.com
- Blurb – www.blurb.com
- BoD (Books on Demand) – www.bod.de
- Book Works - https://www.bookworks.org.uk/
- Bubok – www.bubok.com
- CaféPress – www.cafepress.com
- Casa del Libro – www.casadellibro.com
- CreateSpace – www.createspace.com
- Draft2Digital – www.draft2digital.com
- EPubli.de - http://www.epubli.de/
- Finisterrae Ediciones – www.finisterraediciones.com
- GooglePlay – play.google.com
- iTunesconnect - https://itunesconnect.apple.com/WebObjects/iTunesConnect.woa
- IngramSpark - https://www1.ingramspark.com/Portal
- Kobo Writing Life - http://www.kobo.com/writinglife

- Lighning Source - https://www1.lightningsource.com
- Lulu – www.lulu.com
- Mantra Books - http://www.mantra-books.net/
- Neobooks - http://www.neobooks.com/
- NookPress – www.nookpress.com
- Pubit! – www.pubit.com
- RocaAutores - http://www.rocautores.com/
- SmashWords – www.smashwords.com
- WattPad – www.wattpad.com
- Widbook - http://www.widbook.com/wb/index
- Writers & Artists - https://www.writersandartists.co.uk/self-publishing

Alternative editors and free publishers

- 24Symbols - http://www.24symbols.com/
- BiblioEteca - http://www.biblioeteca.com/
- Biblioteca Digital Hispánica: http://www.bne.es/es/Catalogos/BibliotecaDigital
- CSIC - http://libros.csic.es/freebooks.php
- Europeana - http://www.europeana.eu/
- Librear - http://www.librear.com/
- Librodot - http://www.librodot.com/
- Libroteca - http://www.libroteca.net/
- Open Library - http://openlibrary.org/
- Proyecto Gutemberg - http://www.gutenberg.org/browse/languages/es
- The Internet Archive - https://archive.org/details/texts
- Wikisource - http://es.wikisource.org/wiki/Portada

Crowdfunding

- CrowdFunder - www.crowdfunder.co.uk
- CrowdTilt – www.crowdtilt.com
- FundAnything – http://www.fundanything.com/
- IndieGoGo – http://www.indiegogo.com/
- Kickstarter – www.kickstarter.com

- Lanzanos – www.lanzanos.com
- Pozible - http://www.pozible.com.au/
- StartNext – www.startnext.de
- Verkami – www.verkami.com

Further links…

- IRS – www.irs.gov
- EPUB validator – http://validator.idpf.org
- EpubCheck - https://github.com/IDPF/epubcheck/releases/tag/v3.0.1
- SafeCreative – http://es.safecreative.net
- Goodreads – www.goodreads.com
- Author's blog – http://albertog.over-blog.es
- LinkedIn – www.linkedin.com
- Xing – www.xing.com
- Etsy – www.etsy.com
- Author's web site – www.agbdesign.es
- YouTube – www.youtube.com
- Vimeo – www.vimeo.com
- Wikipedia – www.wikipedia.org
- Amazon Logistics - http://services.amazon.es/servicios/logistica-de-amazon/funciones-y-ventajas.html
- German ISBN agency: www.german-isbn.org

From the same author

Levels and Curves with GIMP (2nd Edition)

Alberto García Briz

ISBN 978-1503229853 (paperback, CreateSpace)

116 pages

Learn to use these two powerful tools with one of the best free applications for image and photo edition. Second edition with extended contents.

Books in Spanish

Blanco y Negro con The GIMP (Spanish)
Alberto García Briz
ISBN 978-1478353911 (paperback, CreateSpace)
232 pages
Learn how to use GIMP in different ways to obtain black and White images with a professional look.
The different techniques are explained step by step through multiple practical examples.

Niveles y Curvas con GIMP 2ed. (Spanish)
Alberto García Briz
ISBN 978-1484813775 (paperback, CreateSpace)
ISBN 978-1502255860 (epub, Draft2Digital)
104 pages
Learn to use these two powerful tools with one of the best free applications for image and photo edition. Second edition (in Spanish) with extended contents.

Publicación online – hazlo tú mismo (Spanish)
Alberto García Briz
ISBN 978-1503186392 (paperback, CreateSpace)
118 pages
Self-publishing is a current trend in Internet. With a few steps, you can have on the table (or in your electronic reader) that book that you kept as draft for years in a drawer...
Fourth edition with extended contents.

Manual básico de Scribus (Spanish)
Alberto García Briz
ISBN 978-1499502442 (paperback, CreateSpace)
ISBN 978-1502250308 (epub, Draft2Digital)
128 pages
Lear to use this powerful, free layout software to produce all kinds of publications with a professional look.

Pequeño diccionario de diseño gráfico y fotografía (Spanish)
ISBN 978-1500140748
40 pages
Terminology used in graphic design and photography is, in many cases, too specific. This book will help you finding your way through them, when working with the different image editors, vector graphics software or layout applications.

Terms and acronyms are explained in a plain, precise words, including, in their case, the explanation of the acronyms and their original language.

This small dictionary compiles and extends the different glossaries included in the different author's books.

Visit our web for further publication updates:

http://www.agbdesign.es/?page_id=5

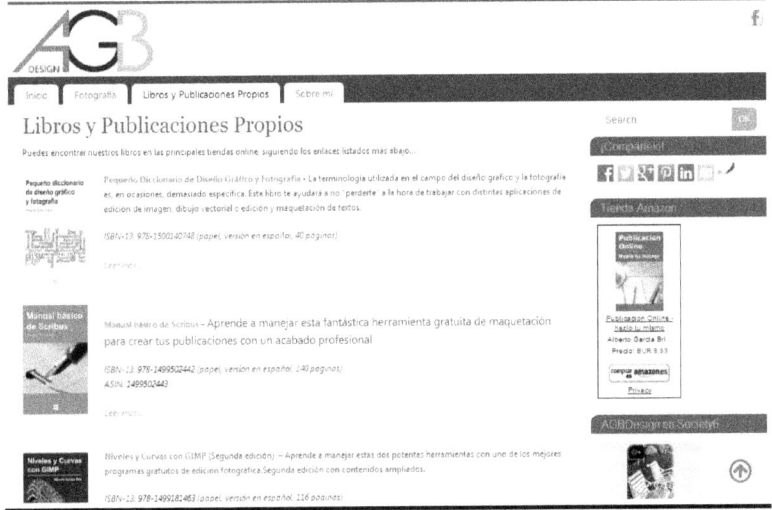

www.ingramcontent.com/pod-product-compliance
Lightning Source LLC
Chambersburg PA
CBHW051218170526
45166CB00005B/1949